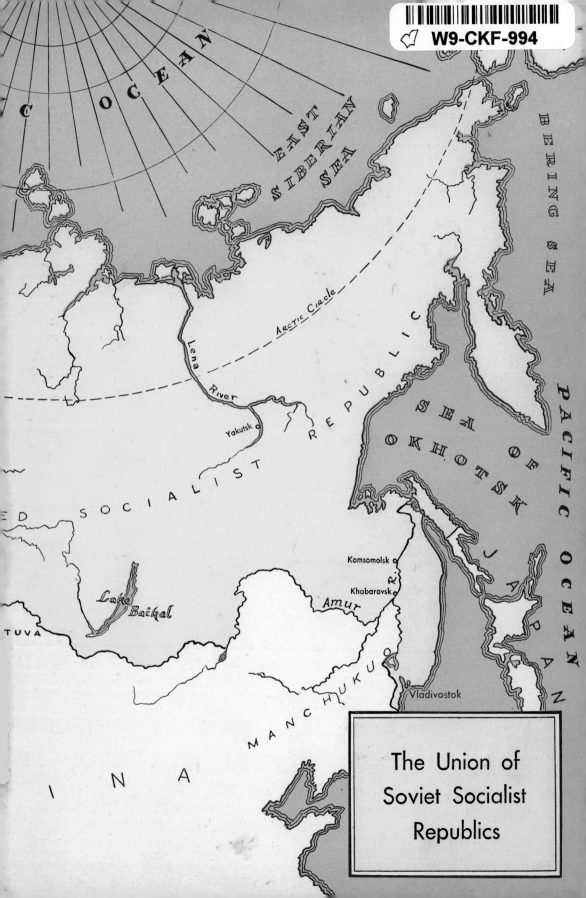

OCEAN

EAST SIBERIAN SEA

BERING SEA

PACIFIC OCEAN

Arctic Circle

Lena River

SEA OF OKHOTSK

J A P A N

Yakutsk

SOCIALIST

REPUBLIC

Komsomolsk

Khabarovsk

Amur R.

Lake Baikal

TUVA

Vladivostok

C H I N A

M A N C H U K U O

The Union of Soviet Socialist Republics

PEOPLES OF THE USSR

By Anna Louise Strong

PEOPLES
of the USSR

By ANNA LOUISE STRONG

Illustrated with photographs

THE MACMILLAN COMPANY · NEW YORK
1944

PRINTED IN THE UNITED STATES OF AMERICA

Permission to use the photographs in this book has been granted to us by Sovfoto, New York.

AUTHOR'S FOREWORD

SOME TWENTY-FIVE YEARS AGO I came to believe, with a few other scattered Americans, that mutual understanding between my native country and the new Russia emerging from the 1917 revolution was of profound importance. To promote such understanding became my life's purpose.

I sought and gladly accepted my first chance to go to Moscow for the American Friends Service in relief work for the Volga famine in 1921. When this work was over I secured assignments from American newspapers and book publishers. For twenty years I succeeded in commuting between New York and Moscow, living in the USSR at least half of every year. I sought not a permanent career with any particular newspaper but a widening knowledge of the Soviet land. I was therefore not confined to immediate news or to residence in Moscow but was often the first or only American to make some unique trip.

My first experience was in the starving city of Samara (now called Kuibyshev) to which I took the first cars of American food and where I remained to organize the first village committees for the wider American Relief Administration. Here, in the heart of Russia, so many children of non-Russian nationality poured into the children's homes that an immediate task was the teaching of a common language to the offspring of a dozen different national groups. This was my earliest glimpse of the many peoples that inhabit the USSR.

In 1922 I camped north of the Arctic Circle in Karelia with the first pioneers who developed the mica mines and feldspar quarries of the north. In the same year I went south to the Donets valley, where Ukrainian miners worked knee-deep in water to reclaim the coal mines; and to Baku, where the chief engineer of the world's richest oil field lived in a two-room tenement with a wife who was ill for lack of proper food. Tiflis, the Georgian capital, managed to be both hospitable and gay even in that hard time of reconstruction. Thus in a single year I saw five different national republics—Russia, the Ukraine, Karelia, Georgia, and Azerbaidjan—struggling to rebuild war-ruined lands. To all of them I returned several years later, when they had had time to rebuild.

My visits to Soviet Central Asia, in 1928, 1929, 1930 and 1940, were also in certain ways unique. At that time foreign correspondents were not admitted to Central Asia. I went there by invitation from the organizations of native women, who wished to know of the world-wide struggle for women's rights.

The following year I camped in the felt tents of the Kirghiz, traveling into the high Pamirs where Americans and English-men in the past have penetrated but rarely. Thus I saw the old nomad life in the decade before it vanished from the USSR.

I went again the next year to Central Asia, this time to the opening of the Turkestan-Siberian Railway, the north-south line through Asia that changed forever the life of a continent. When the other press correspondents went back by the southern route, as they had come, I transferred to the jerky but adven-turous "special" that took delegates north to Siberia, the first train to make the through trip. In Siberia I saw the beginnings of the now famous steel city, Kuznetsk.

In this growing life of the USSR I took part not only as observer but sometimes as participant. In the years after the Volga famine I helped organize a farm colony of homeless chil-dren, the John Reed Colony on the Volga, using my annual trips to America to secure funds and farm machinery.

Thousands of Americans came to the USSR in 1930 and thereafter to work in the mighty construction jobs of the Five Year Plan. For them I organized the *Moscow News*, at first a weekly and then a daily, the first English-language newspaper in the USSR. As its managing editor I met Stalin in a small committee meeting that remains the most important single experience of my life. In that short hour I saw how decisions are reached in the Soviet Union and how the USSR is held together —not by orders of a dictator but by arousing the ideas, initiative, and will of many people and combining them to a common end. The world saw this in the second World War.

The changing world situation took me in 1936 and thereafter from America to Spain and China in several successive trips. These trips were always en route to Moscow. For I had married a Russian and Moscow was our home. Yet for me America was home also. I worked for America and my citizenship remained American. For the ten years of our marriage I was privileged to see the USSR and the world not only through my own eyes, which will always be American, but through my husband's eyes—those of a Soviet editor and reporter.

In 1940 I returned to Moscow, intending to remain. I reached Italy on the last American boat, got out of that country two days ahead of her declaration of war, passed through Berlin at the time when the German Press Department was inviting correspondents to visit "conquered London in a few weeks," and reached the Baltic States the week the Red Army marched in.

Knowing the world importance of the changes I saw in those small countries, I remained for a month—the only American correspondent in the Baltic States during the weeks they were becoming Soviet Republics. Three months later I left Moscow by train for Alma Ata, where I took plane for China—the first American to travel by that new trans-Asia air line. In thus returning to America—by plane above the Japanese lines to Hongkong—I was the first wartime traveler around the world across both battle fronts.

AUTHOR'S FOREWORD

It was my Soviet husband, during that last residence in Moscow, who made me understand that my place was in my own country during its entrance into war. "I'll not expect you in 1941," he told me, "but perhaps in 1942." But before 1942 was far advanced he was one of those Soviet civilians—they were tragically but gloriously many—who worked themselves to death for our common victory. He rose from a sickbed on the news of the Hitler invasion, plunged into feverish work for better relations with the Anglo-Saxon countries, and continued without rest until he died.

So in preparing this book for American young people I continue not only my own work but his. I cannot hope that it will convey all that we saw and felt of the vigor, vitality, and importance of those many different Soviet peoples who share with all of us the postwar world. But I hope it may at least introduce American youth to an appreciation of how vast is the variety of human beings who, in their many ways, take part in the great quest for life, liberty, and happiness.

I think I am thus far the only American who has visited fifteen of the sixteen Soviet Republics. But I shall not be the last.

I mail this Foreword not from my California home but from a Montana airport as I leave on one more historic trip—by airplane from the very heart of the North American continent, through Canada, Alaska, Siberia, to Moscow—the heart of the USSR. Thus go the lend-lease planes, knitting together the two great nations.

By this new route I am one of the first Americans to travel. But for our postwar world it is the great international airway of the Northern Hemisphere.

ANNA LOUISE STRONG

Airport in Montana, June 13, 1944

CONTENTS

WHO ARE THE SOVIET PEOPLE?

THE SECOND WORLD WAR made everyone ask it. What is the USSR? Who are these people that we once called Russians? Even their chief of state, Stalin, comes from a country called Georgia, and is not a Russian at all.

Twenty-eight men thrust their bodies against tanks in the days when Hitler almost entered Moscow. From the northwest the German tanks came onward by a frost-hard road. The German High Command declared that they could see the Kremlin spires; they would enter the Soviet capital in a single drive. Beyond the seas a hushed world waited, predicting Moscow's fall.

I

Stalin said to General Panfilov: "Hold the northwest road at any cost." The men of Panfilov's division were not all Russians. They were heavily diluted with yellow-skinned men of the east —Kirghiz and Kazakhs, who twenty-five years ago had massacred Russians and whom the Russians had slaughtered in their turn. How could you trust such men with the defense of Moscow?

Twenty-eight men held a point on the road. They were attacked by twenty German tanks. . . . "Come on, boys; that's less than a tank apiece," shouted one of the men. They blew up the tanks with hand grenades. Thirty more tanks came on. One by one the twenty-eight died at their post. But they stopped fifty tanks and held the road till relief arrived. Moscow hailed them, saying: "They died, but still they won."

Who are these people who fought so heroically? They call themselves the "Soviet people"; the word "soviet" means "council" and designates the form of their elected government. They call their country the "Union of Soviet Socialist Republics"—USSR or Soviet Union for short. With the new name there seems to have appeared a new nation—or league of nations —that is certainly much stronger than before. Less than thirty years ago the nation called Russia was first to crack under the strain of the first World War. What is this new nation or league of nations? Whence is its unexpected strength?

The USSR is the world's largest country; it includes about one-sixth of all the dry land of the earth. It is about the size of all of North America; it is more than twice as large as our United States. The summer sun never sets on the great extent of it. When the long June days draw to a close in Leningrad at nine o'clock in the evening, it is already seven o'clock next morning in Kamchatka on the Pacific and the sun of the next day has been up for several hours. Each New Year, arriving, is greeted ten times as it travels across the country. The Far Eastern Express takes nine days from Moscow to Vladivostok. In the Vladivostok station stands a post marked "9329 km" (5789 miles); there is no such figure on a milepost anywhere else in the world.

The USSR is also one of the world's most populous countries; it contains one-eleventh part of all the people in the world. Only China and India surpass it in population; it has half again as many people as our United States. Its 192,695,000 inhabitants include over 100 distinct nationalities and peoples speaking 125 different languages. Books, textbooks, and newspapers have to be printed in all these languages in the USSR.

The people of the USSR are the world's youngest people. More than half of them are under twenty-five. In this they resemble the America of fifty years ago or earlier, boiling with young energies that attacked the wilderness. The Soviet population's youth is partly due, as in early America, to hardships that shortened the life of older people in previous years. It is due still more to the high birth rate combined with a falling death rate.

The USSR has every kind of landscape. There are thousands of miles of virgin forests and thousands of miles of treeless plains. Some of the world's highest mountains are found here; Mt. Elbrus in the Caucasus, 18,468 feet high, is the highest mountain in Europe; Stalin Peak in the Pamirs is 24,590 feet high and surpassed only by the great Himalayas of India, which lie beyond it to the south. In the Soviet Pamirs lie some of the world's highest settlements, over 13,000 feet above sea level. But the USSR has also the world's lowest cities. Baku, Astrakhan, and Krasnovodsk, on the Caspian, are all below the level of the sea.

Great deserts of sand are found in the Soviet Union; there

3

are also thousands of lakes, among them the world's deepest, Lake Baikal, and the world's largest landlocked body of water, the Caspian—so large that it is called not a lake but a sea. Of the world's ten longest rivers, four—the Ob, Amur, Lena, and Yenesei—are found in the USSR. So are the world's longest non-Arctic glaciers, Fedshenko in the Pamirs and the South Inilshek in the Tien Shan, each nearly fifty miles long.

The USSR has great extremes of climate. The world's coldest spot is not at the North Pole but in eastern Siberia near the city of Verkhoyansk, where 95 below zero (Fahrenheit) has been registered. Few spots on earth are hotter than the sunstruck sands of Turkmenia, where at 185 degrees you can cook eggs with the heat of sand and sun. Over the Bering Sea the fog may last for weeks, while over the Kara-kum desert in Turkmenia there is not a single wisp of cloud for months. At Batum in western Georgia more rain falls in a single downpour than in a whole year near the Aral Sea.

These extremes of climate and conditions produce extremes of vegetation. The larch trees on the shores of Okhotsk Sea opposite Alaska take a hundred years to grow as thick as a baby's fist; the young bamboo of southern Georgia grows a foot and a half in a single day. The wild plants of the USSR vary from Arctic lichens and mosses to subtropical palms and lotus flowers; the birds, from Arctic owls to flamingos; the wild animals, from polar bears to tigers. The soil varies from the eternally frozen subsoil of the tundra to the rich black earth of grain-bearing prairies and the fertile red earth of Colchis in western Georgia, which produces three harvests a year.

The variety of climate demands great variety in farming. The water-loving rice and the drought-resistant sorghum are both grown on Soviet soil. In northern Russia farms are made by clearing away the trees. Southeast of the Volga a belt of trees

Reindeer teams of the frozen North contrast with tropical foliage along the Black Sea—all within the wide stretches of the USSR

a thousand miles long is being planted from the Azov Sea to the spurs of the Urals to protect the farms from dry winds; 840,000 acres were thus planted in 1933–1938.

The natural resources of the USSR are greater and more varied than those of any other country. Soviet geologists claim for their land more than half the world's known deposits of oil, iron, and peat, and 21 per cent of the world's coal. Such claims are tentative, for much of the world's reserves is still unknown; some 85 per cent of Soviet resources have been discovered only in recent years. Soviet geological oil deposits are figured at 6376 million tons, peat at 150,000 million tons, coal at 1654 billion tons, ordinary iron ore at 10,600 million tons—while, with the addition of the famous Kursk anomaly, there is the incredible total of 267,000 million tons of iron ore and quartzites.

The potential water power of Soviet rivers is estimated at 280 million kilowatts, 28 per cent of the world total, which puts the USSR ahead of any other country. The USSR's two and a half billion acres of trees form one-third of all the world's forests. Its croplands are larger than those of any other nation, the area actually harvested in 1939 being over 334 million acres; the United States comes next, with about 321 million.

It is clear that the USSR has many striking resemblances— in size and variety of resources—to the United States of America. In the past this similarity has not been widely noticed, for old Russia developed much more slowly than America did. Its resources were not explored; its farming was primitive; its industries were scanty and foreign-owned. Since the Russian Revolution of 1917 the country has developed at a speed greater than that of America, since it has much farther to go. Its farms have been mechanized; the output of its industry in 1939 was nine times what it was in 1928. Travelers in recent years to the USSR have noticed more and more the likeness between its people and the American people, in problems and technical methods. In part this is because the Soviet people have consciously copied America; in part, because their land presents a challenge similar to ours.

Their land, like ours, is a melting pot of many nations. The people are today a pioneering people, eager to exploit their untapped wealth. Their farms are great farms, even larger than American farms, quite different from the small handicraft farms of Europe. "Russians and Americans farm; the little nations of Europe garden," said an expert of the U.S. Department of Agriculture on seeing the great wheat fields of Siberia, serviced by tractors and harvest combines. The Soviet people are well aware of these similarities. For the past twenty years America is the only land they have ever taken as a model. To work "po Amerikanski"—American style—is high praise in their industrial technique.

How did it happen that these energetic people, owning so vast a territory, have only recently begun its full development? Why was this great land so easily beaten in the first World War? The reasons lie in part in a peculiarity of the land's geography and still more in its history for the past two thousand years.

The geographical peculiarity of this country is that it is backed against the North Pole. Southward it faces both Europe and Asia, but its great bulk lies farther north than any other great country; its Arctic coast lies nearer the pole than the northernmost part of the American continent. Some 16 per cent of its territory is in the cold zone, where the subsoil is forever frozen, while 50 per cent consists of a great forest zone stretching from east to west across the country's whole expanse. It is a harsh land, for much of it is hard to develop.

It is also hard for these people to reach the world's great trade routes and to mix in the expanding life of the world.

The USSR has, it is true, a tremendously long frontier—36,000 miles—two-thirds of which fronts salt water. Its land frontier touches a dozen foreign states. Its shore line is almost as long as the equator; it is washed by twelve seas, parts of three great oceans. This would seem to insure easy outlet in all directions. But eight of these seas lie north of the Arctic Circle and are frozen most of the year. The other four—the Caspian, Black, Azov, and Baltic—are largely or entirely land-locked, any outlets to the ocean being held by other world powers. On the land side the USSR is shut off from most of its neighbors by great mountains and wide deserts. Most of its long rivers flow into the frozen ocean or into inland seas.

The entire territory is thus the heart of the earth's great land masses, with no easy way to reach the sea. During the long ages when men traveled by caravan, the southern part of this country lay on the highway of the world's life. In recent centuries, with the rise of sea trade, this land has been shut out from the great trade routes and its history has been marked by an urge to reach some warm port on an open sea. Today, and tomorrow, with the development of the airplane and the conquest of the Arctic, the USSR's geographical position gains an importance that it lacked before.

A glance at a polar map contains many surprises that revolutionize our view of world geography. We see that the great bulk of land—and this means of people—lies in the Northern Hemisphere around the North Pole. The shortest air line from New York to Chungking, China, or to any point in India, lies directly over the pole. The shortest sea route from San Francisco to Hongkong and India passes up the coast of Alaska and down the coast of the USSR. Dutch Harbor in the Aleutians and Petropavlovsk on Kamchatka seem to most of us very distant, but they actually lie on the shortest route. Hitherto they have been avoided because of their bad climate, but future long-distrance stratosphere flying will go that way.

Even today the USSR is one of our closest neighbors. Little Diomede Island, a possession of the United States in the Bering Strait, is only five miles from Big Diomede, which belongs to the USSR: In the future ways of the air our nearness to the USSR will become much more evident and more important. The USSR, the U.S.A., and Canada dominate the polar routes. Only through the purchase of Alaska eighty years ago from old Russia can the United States claim her port on tomorrow's central ways of the air.

The Soviet land holds nearly half the circle of the Arctic. It reaches south 3600 miles to the Hindukush at the gates of India. It stretches 5400 miles from west to east, from the Baltic to the Bering Sea. The Soviet people are all the tribes and nations that have been living in this vast area from long before history, that have fought and conquered and enslaved one another for centuries but that now have built a strong and modern union on the base of a common heritage.

THE LONG PAST

THE EARLIEST HOME OF MAN, the original "garden of Eden," probably lay in or near the region that is Soviet Central Asia today. The Vale of Kashmir to the south in India, the oases of Chinese Turkestan to the east, and the valley of the Amu, or Oxus, to the west bear traces of man's early life.

As years passed and the Glacial Age receded, the heart of Asia grew drier and hotter. Some men fought the growing drought; others fled from it. Those who fought the drought became the world's first settled farmers and most-ancient civilizations: in Babylonia, Assyria, Central Asia, China. Those who fled the drying lands established the countries of Europe and of our modern world.

The home-staying folk in the heart of Asia learned to irrigate with water from mountain streams and rivers. They made houses of sun-dried clay. They made crude plows of heavy wooden sticks drawn by oxen, such as we see in pictures of Biblical times. They grew barley and rice, cultivated vineyards and orchards. For clothing they raised cotton or cultivated silkworms for silk. They organized states out of which grew great empires. The small states arose because men needed to control the irrigation water. The empires took tribute from smaller states and protected the trade routes, so that caravans of camels might carry goods from land to land.

At the edge of all these ancient civilizations lived nomad peoples, hunters and tamers of cattle, wandering from one grassy spot to another in the mountain pastures or in the thin growth of the deserts. Their food was milk and meat; their wealth was in their herds. They wore skins and furs; they camped in felt tents made by the women from the wool of sheep and camels. They tamed wild horses and rode them from camp to camp and to give battle. For they looked with envious eyes on the fat crops by the rivers. They followed the caravan tracks and looted the traders. When they were strong enough, they conquered the farming civilizations and took over the cities; then they either mingled with the people they had conquered or rode on to loot other cities and farms. The greatest number of these nomads, these traveling people, lived in the wide belt of grasslands that stretches from Mongolia westward across all of Asia, across the Ukraine, and even into Poland.

The roads by which the tribes traveled into Europe became the highways of history. The earliest tribes went by the southern oases, circling south of the Caspian, and came at last to the lands of Asia Minor, where Armenia, Georgia, and Turkey are today. These lands were settled so long ago that we cannot even guess the earliest date of their history. Later tribes traveled the belt of grasslands south of the Urals, to settle northern Europe, or turned south into the Danube valley and eventually peopled Greece and Rome and Spain.

Still other tribes traveled by the great Siberian rivers, whose tributaries interlock so that there is easy portage from one river to the next. Some drifted downstream to a dead end at the Arctic; these dwindled into the Arctic peoples of today. Others, the luckier ones, kept ever westward until they reached the Baltic, where the craft they had learned on the rivers made them rovers of the sea. They peopled the Scandinavian lands and kept onward into the Atlantic, discovering Iceland, Greenland, and the coast of North America.

In this long story of Asia and Europe the story of the Soviet land and people has its place. Their land is the territory that was crossed by all the great migrations, whether by the southern oases, the middle grasslands, or the northern river route. Their people are the children of the scores of tribes or tribal remnants that for one reason or another did not push on into Europe but remained to people the southern oases, the wide belt of prairies, the forests of the north.

Their history falls into two separate cycles: the story of the people of the sunny lands of irrigated oases and foothills and the story of the northern folk of the rivers and woods. Only in the nineteenth century, with the Russian conquest of Trans-Caucasia and Central Asia, did these two stories become one.

The people who today form the Soviet Republics in Asia have a common history. They lived along the southern caravan route from China to Iran and the Mediterranean. Their farming was based on irrigation; their civilization developed early. They were the discoverers of the uses of bronze and, later, iron.

THE LONG PAST

The Roman Empire at the height of its power reached as far as the Caspian Sea and held the lands that are today Armenia, Georgia, and Azerbaidjan. Far to the east the first great empire of China had arisen under the dynasty of the Han. In the first century of the Christian era Chinese troops carried the rule of the Han across the oases of Turkestan until fifty "kings" paid tribute. A Chinese army of 70,000 under Pan Chao reached the eastern shore of the Caspian, separated only by its waters from the Roman Empire. Pan Chao knew of the existence of the Roman Empire; he sent an envoy to contact it, but the Parthian guides misled the envoy and brought him south to the Persian Gulf. How could the Chinese envoy know the difference? It was long before the days of maps!

Trade of those days, however, passed through these boundaries. Chinese silk, jade, lacquer, and art products penetrated all the sunny lands of Asia, and crossed to the western limits of the Roman Empire.

The Silk Road today—this ancient highway connected the civilizations of China and the Roman Empire

During the long centuries of the Roman Empire's decline in the west (in A.D. 395 it was divided into Eastern and Western Empires) there appeared a new force stronger than conquest or trade as a unifier of peoples. It was the influence of a common religion. Missionaries from the Church of Rome penetrated northward among the barbarian tribes, carrying the laws and learning of Rome; thus modern Europe came into existence, cherishing, despite all wars, a common tradition of thought. Missionaries from the Eastern Empire penetrated northward among the barbarian tribes of today's Russia, unifying the people around the law and learning of Greece.

Far to the south in the dingy little town of Medina, Arabia, there appeared a man who sent envoys in A.D. 629 to the courts of the three great empires—to the Persian emperor, the emperor at Constantinople, and Emperor Tai-tsung of the Tang Dynasty in China—calling upon them all to follow "Muhammed, the prophet of God." The brilliant and tolerant Chinese emperor answered politely, the answer from Constantinople is unrecorded, but the Persian emperor tore up the letter and flung the pieces at the envoy. Persia had Zoroastrianism, a fire-worshiping religion of its own.

"Even so, O Lord!" cried the angry man in Medina. "Rend Thou his kingdom from him!" With the help of Muhammed's followers the Lord, whom they called Allah, did. The Arabs conquered Persia within twenty-five years. In a little more than a century, by A.D. 750, the Moslem Empire ruled all the peoples of the sunny lands from the borders of India and China through Turkestan, Persia, Syria, Egypt and northern Africa, and far into Spain. On all these lands the Moslems imposed their religion. Only Armenia and Georgia remained Christian.

In those days the Arab civilization was higher than that of Europe. Arabs knew astronomy and mathematics; they invented the system of numerals that we use today. They studied physiology and hygiene; their surgeons performed difficult operations, using anesthetics. Much of the Arab learning was considered a "black art" by the Church of the Middle Ages; the practice of medicine was discouraged by some churchmen, the sick being expected to seek relief through prayer. The Arabs practiced scientific farming, used fertilizer, knew how to graft trees and produce new types of fruit and flowers. They traded with highly civilized China, which under the Tang Dynasty was one of the most splendid empires the world has ever seen. Arabs reached it not only by caravan but by sea around India. All the inventions of China and Arabia, including paper for writing, reached the peoples who today form the Soviet Republics of Asia. They were united by the culture of the Arabs and by the religion of Muhammed, the Arabian "prophet of God."

The horsemen of Genghiz Khan destroyed all these civilizations in the thirteenth century. The military genius of their leader organized them into a ruthless, fast-riding horde of cavalry whose conquests were the most rapid and remarkable the world has ever seen. They gained their victories not by weight of numbers but by brilliant strategy. Their territory reached from Hungary and Poland across Asia to the Pacific Ocean and southward to the Persian Gulf. But they brought no new religion; Moslems remained Moslems.

Tamerlane rose in Central Asia in the fourteenth century, established his capital at Samarkand, and became one of the great emperors of history. Thirty wars of conquest brought under his rule all the sunny lands of Central Asia, Iran, and India as far as the Ganges, Syria, and much of Asia Minor. Even southern Russia as far as Moscow paid him a distant tribute.

All these great civilizations were doomed to decay through an event that seemed, at the time, a mere trifle. A small band of

Central Asian herdsmen fled before the invasions of Genghiz Khan and came after many wanderings to Asia Minor, where they grew strong in fighting. They were the Ottoman Turks. In 1453 they took Constantinople, the capital of the Eastern Empire, which had survived by a thousand years the western half of the ancient empire of Rome. With the fall of this city to the uncultured barbarians and the flight of the Christian learned men to the north and west, the link between Asia and Europe was broken.

Man's onward march, halted in one direction, went forward in another. In 1492, fifty years after the fall of Constantinople blocked the land route, Christopher Columbus, a seaman of the Mediterranean, sought India by sea and found America.

Even before this a Slav prince in a town of log houses by a northern river, who ruled a considerable number of similar log towns in the clearings of the woods, had married a princess of the no-longer-existent Eastern Empire, declared himself the protector of the empire's Orthodox Christianity and the rightful heir to the title "Caesar" or "Tsar." He adopted the double eagle, the ancient emblem of the empire, and set up a court modeled on the splendor of the old Greek court. He invited Italian craftsmen and painters to build him a fine castle of brick and stone surrounded by a moat.

He was Ivan the Third, prince of Moscow; he built the Kremlin towers, which still remain.

THE RUSSIAN EMPIRE

THE SLAV PRINCE, Ivan the Third, who snatched the regalia of dead Caesars to enhance his renown came from a different past. Just when or how the Slav tribes, the northern folk of the long rivers and the deep woods, came from the birthplace of races in Asia is unrecorded.

They built log cabins in forest clearings, protecting their families and livestock from wild beasts by earthen walls or wooden stockades. They hunted for food and furs, domesticated bees for honey, made little farms by burning down trees and scattering seed on soil mixed with ashes. Later they invented a wooden plow with metal tip; it was called "sokha" and was a slight advance on the wooden stick-plows of Central Asia. They exchanged goods in trading towns that grew up along the rivers, for there were few roads in the woods.

By the ninth century the Slavs had many trading towns ruled by princes and town councils of landlords and merchants, without whom the prince could not make war. Most of the towns lay along a trade route that led from the Baltic southward by river, crossed by portage to the headwaters of the Dnieper, and so came southward to the Greek towns on the Black Sea. The most important towns were Novgorod, near the northern end of the route and fortified against the sea rovers of the Baltic, and Kiev, at the southern end of the forests just before the great river entered the prairie country where riverfolk had to fear the horsemen of the plains.

Sea rovers of the Baltic seized Novgorod in the ninth century —the same century in which these same Danes or Vikings were plundering the coasts of King Alfred of England. The sea rovers were quite at home on the river trade route; they kept on south and conquered Kiev. They mixed with the Slav tribes and adopted their language, much as the Danish raiders mixed with the people of Britain. They led the Slav tribes in a campaign against Constantinople, which was then the capital of the Eastern Empire, ruled by Greeks. The Greek Emperor bought peace by paying a huge ransom in gold, costly fabrics, and slaves. He signed a trade treaty with Kiev-Russ, which thus emerged, in A.D. 911, with its new name, a respectable member of the family of nations.

Prince Vladimir of Kiev-Russ married the Greek Emperor's sister and adopted the Christian religion in A.D. 988. He destroyed the images of nature gods—the sun, the wind, and the thunder—and ordered the people of Kiev to enter the Dnieper while Greek priests from Constantinople read prayers and declared them all baptized. Christian shrines replaced the pagan idols in the market towns along the river; churches and monasteries followed. Kiev became "Holy Kiev, mother of Russian cities"; Vladimir's armies put down any who opposed.

Thus the Slav people inherited Greek civilization and an alphabet based on the Greek. Christian monasteries became centers of learning; they followed wherever the Russian traders went. So, while western Europe lay in the shadow of the Dark Ages, the culture of old Greece flowed northward into Russia. This was both fortune and misfortune. The Christian religion and civilization that came with it helped weld the scattered Slav tribes into a nation. But it separated them from Europe, from the Middle Ages down to the present, by the barrier of a different church and a different alphabet. Europe derived its simpler alphabets from the Roman. Europeans stared at the richer, more varied alphabet of the Russians—which came from Greece, the fount of Europe's culture—and called the Russians strange, a race apart.

For more than two centuries—1240–1480—the Russians tasted the humiliation of the conquered. They were forced to pay tribute to a Mongol state on the lower Volga whose tribesmen were known as the Golden Horde, of whom an Arab writer wrote: "I never saw a people with more beautifully built bodies, tall like palm trees, with blond hair. Each of them has many kinds of knives and swords; their women wear many strands of beads and colored ribbons. They are cheerful and hospitable and often have great competitions of songs and dances." His description would be recognized today.

The Russians who finally beat the Mongols were rallied around a new center. Moscow was born in a cluster of log houses surrounded by a wooden stockade. It was first heard of as a village in A.D. 1147. A century or so later it was burned down by the Mongols; but it soon revived, being too far in the woods for regular visits from the Golden Horde. Two or three clever—and quite unscrupulous—princes in the fourteenth to sixteenth century rapidly made Moscow the head of a powerful state.

Ivan the Fourth, known as Ivan the Terrible—a word applied in compliment to his many victories—was the cleverest of these three princes. He was considered a madman by many, and possibly was; but he made Russia one of the largest states in the world. He collected the pieces of the Golden Horde's scattered empire along the Volga, thus owning the trade route to Asia. Princes north of the Caucasus at once offered tribute and the Russian state began to contain non-Russian nationalities. Ivan established the first printing shop in Moscow as a strictly supervised propaganda office of his government.

His cleverest act, by which he most influenced history, was the deal in 1581 with the outlaw Yermak, chief of a band of several thousand men. These freemen were called Cossacks; the nobles considered them outlaws and put a price on their heads, but Ivan the Terrible found a better use for them—to extend the lands of the Russian state.

Ivan got rid of Yermak's Cossack band, which was causing unrest on the southeastern border, by offering them as much free land in Siberia as they could take from the Mongol khan. They entered Siberia in 1581, conquered the khan, and took his wealth. Yermak, the first Siberian, died, but the Cossacks drove on. They journeyed swiftly westward by the great tributaries of Siberian rivers, building forts at the portages, lured by the profits of the fur trade and the freedom of the life. Behind them came other hunters and trappers, merchants, priests and monks, and eventually settlers.

Fifty-eight years after the Cossacks started east, Russians were building log houses on the shores of the Pacific and looking with interest at Alaska. They had crossed all of Asia in little

more than half a century, nearly twice as far as the width of
North America. That was the same half century in which British seamen defeated the Spanish Armada (1588) and British
colonists landed in North America (1608 in Virginia and 1620
at Plymouth). Those were the years in which the nations of
Europe wore themselves out in the Thirty Years' War. In that
half century Great Britain became the world's greatest sea
power, Russia became the world's greatest land power, and a
new world—America—was born.

Yet, as people in western Europe and America forged ahead
through new discoveries, Russia was seen to be lagging behind.
Its upper class suppressed all new ideas, lest these undermine
their rule. They even followed the traditions of Asia acquired
through long centuries under the Golden Horde. Nobles wore
long beards and long robes; they often veiled their wives, forbidding them to speak to men outside their family, but the
peasant women never adopted this eastern custom.

Peter the Great (1672–1725) hated the Asiatic customs of
his nobles; he admired the rising sea power of Great Britain.
Russia was the largest land power, but it had no port facing
Europe. The Black Sea coasts were held by Turkey, while the
Baltic coasts between Russia and the sea belonged to Sweden,
which had a fine navy and the best army in the world. Russia
faced only toward Asia; to trade with Britain she had to use
Archangel, an inconvenient port facing the Arctic and frozen
most of the year. Peter thought Russia would advance faster if
it had better connection with Europe.

So Peter made plans. He went abroad to Holland and England, then the most advanced European powers. He studied
armies and navies. The nobles tried to overthrow him in his
absence; the heads of the Orthodox Church denounced a tsar
who worked with his hands. Peter came back and put down the

nobles and declared that henceforth the tsar was the head of the Church. He was copying Henry the Eighth of England, who had lived over a century before.

Then Peter fought Sweden persistently for twenty-one years. At first he was badly beaten, but he learned from every defeat and finally won. He took from Sweden part of the Baltic coast, including the swampy mouth of the Neva. Here he built a fortress, a port, and a city; it was called Petersburg. Peter made it his capital, though it was inconveniently far away from most of Russia. It was his "window on Europe."

Peter achieved his object of bringing Russia closer to Europe. He made the Russian Empire greater and the nobles and merchants grew more prosperous. But the lot of the common people grew even harder through heavier taxes and increasing serfdom. There were many serf rebellions against Peter, but he suppressed them and executed the leaders. So the great and growing empire kept a weakness at its core. Many of Peter's most brilliant ideas—the Moscow-Volga Canal, the Arctic sea route around Asia, the shifting of the river Amu back to the Caspian—slumbered after his death for more than two centuries and were realized only after Lenin and Stalin aroused the common people whom Peter forgot.

Catherine the Second, a German princess who came to the Russian throne in 1762 by marriage and the murder of her husband, posed as an enlightened despot. She became famous as a patroness of liberal ideas. But when those ideas were expressed in the American Revolution, the horrified Catherine at once denounced those "godless folk who deny the divine right of kings." She was still more shocked by the French Revolution, since it was nearer Russia.

Catherine's generals took the Crimea from the Turks. Poland also was conquered and divided among Russia, Prussia, and Austria. In 1794 Poland ceased to exist as an independent state and was not revived for more than a hundred years. All these wars and the brilliance of Catherine's court had to be paid for. Taxes and dues to the state increased fivefold during her reign. Catherine gave away more than a million peasants—they were serfs of the state—to her favorites.

The greatest of all the peasant wars broke out against Catherine. It was led by Emelian Pugachev, a Cossack of the southern prairies; he was joined by peasants and by native peoples of the Volga. Serf workers in the Ural ironworks made guns for him. In 1773 rumors ran through Moscow that Pugachev was coming to free all serfs. Many Moscow merchants hoped for this because small merchants were oppressed by big ones. Pugachev was defeated; he was brought to Moscow in chains in a cage and executed in a public square in January, 1775.

Three months after this fighter for freedom was killed in Russia, the first shots of the American Revolution rang out in Concord and Lexington. Fourteen years later the people of Paris stormed the Bastille and set the prisoners free. The great revolutions that made the modern world had begun.

Russia's ruling class from Catherine onward set itself bitterly against these changes, which would have robbed them of their feudal privileges. While America and Europe swept forward into the tremendous progress of the nineteenth century, Russia of the tsars and feudal nobles became known as the persecutor of every liberal thought, the bulwark of every reactionary clique in Europe, the prisonhouse of the common people.

Throughout the nineteenth century many able men strove in various ways to reform the autocratic tsardom and corrupt bureaucracy. Some were brilliant writers. Alexander Pushkin, Russia's most famous poet, wrote poems of freedom that were copied by hand and circulated in secret. Many of the great

Russian writers won lasting world fame. Nikolai Gogol is known for his scathing satires, Ivan Turgenev wrote *Fathers and Sons* about the conflict between the old and the new; most famous of all was Leo Tolstoy, whose writings sternly condemned the tyranny of tsarist officials and nobles but who was himself an important noble too well known abroad for the tsar to suppress. His novels are read throughout the world.

Many brilliant musicians appeared in Russia during the nineteenth century. Even composers who said nothing at all in words against the tsar were persecuted if they appeared to exalt the common folk. Michael Glinka composed the first Russian opera, *Ruslan and Ludmilla*, using the music of Russian folk songs and of other nationalities living in Russia. The aristocracy so despised his work that he left Russia and died in a foreign land. Today he is known as the father of Russian music, the first of a brilliant line which contains Moussorgsky, Rimsky-Korsakov, Borodin, Tschaikovsky, and today's Shostakovich.

In 1861, under the influence of the American Civil War and fearing a peasants' war in Russia, Alexander the Second issued a manifesto freeing the peasants from serfdom. The peasants could no longer be bought and sold; they were no longer property. But they were granted little land, and they had to pay for this at high rates which took forty years to repay. Besides, the nobles kept the rights to the forests, the meadows, and the pastures; the peasants could use them only on the landlords' terms. Farming continued to be very primitive, in the style of the Middle Ages. One-third of all the peasants had only a single horse, while another third had no horse at all. Under such conditions it is clear that farming could not advance.

America and Europe went forward rapidly into the nineteenth and twentieth centuries. People learned to read and write; modern machinery came and the standard of living rose.

But Russia of the tsars remained in the Middle Ages. The great masses of people could not read. The countryside was sunk in superstition. The bureaucracy and the Church were corrupt and ignorant. When the first farm tractors appeared in the rural districts—most of them came after the Revolution—the priests led the peasants to stone them as "devil machines."

Thus Russia fell behind in the race for human progress. Her backwardness at last was shown in war. The first sign was in the Crimean War of 1853, when Russia went to war against Turkey to get the Dardanelles. England and France declared war on Russia and entered the Black Sea with battleships driven by steam against a Russian fleet of sailing ships; their heavy guns had twice the range of the Russians'. The tsar's officialdom was so inefficient that his generals did not even have good maps of their own Crimea.

Smarting under his defeat, the Russian tsar sent his armies into Central Asia to restore his lost prestige and to seize the Central Asian cotton lands. Thousands of Russian peasants died in the two-thousand-mile trek over waterless plains, for which they were badly prepared. But in 1865 they took Tashkent, largest city of Central Asia; three years later they conquered Samarkand, once the famous capital of Tamerlane. The conquest moved eastward into the rich Fergana valley; the people fought with knives and pikes but were soon subdued. A few years later the fringes of the land were conquered, the Turkmenian deserts and the Kirghiz mountain pastures.

So the peoples of the sunny lands, the Uzbeks, the Tadjiks, the Kirghiz, the Turkmenians, who had lived there long before the Russians and been part of most of the great world empires, came under the Russian Empire. The cotton country—the land of "white gold"—fell into the hands of the tsar's officers and the Russian industrialists. It was called "Russian Turkestan, the brightest jewel in the crown of empire," copying the words the British use of India. Giddy fortunes were made in cotton lands by the officers. They forgot, in this profitable conquest of weaker peoples, that they had proved unfit to war with European powers. Outwardly the Russian Empire reached its zenith, but its inner tensions increased through the addition of millions of unwilling subjects of a different race.

In 1905 Russia was beaten by Japan, who attacked without declaration of war and swiftly routed the tsar's army. The sufferings and disillusion of the Russian people led to uprisings of peasants and workers great enough to be called a revolution; the tsardom's bureaucracy learned from it only to be more oppressive than before.

In 1914 the German Kaiser attacked Russia. He used against the Russians only 85 of his 220 divisions, keeping 135 for his more difficult western front. He contented himself with taking Poland and most of the Baltic coast and shutting off the rest of Russia by a barrier of barbed wire while he gave his attention to Great Britain, France, and the United States. Those 85 divisions were enough to bring the great Russian Empire to collapse and revolution. For behind that barbed wire the country with the world's largest crop area began to starve. It starved for lack of man power, of tools, of transport. It starved through inner disorganization and decay.

Revolt first started among the native peoples of Central Asia. That is their proud boast today—the revolt that spread from the Caspian to the Chinese border in 1916. They said in Tashkent: "We were the first! A whole year sooner than Moscow or Petersburg." It was a naïve boast. The tsar sent several divisions from the front and suppressed that revolt as ruthlessly and as successfully as in the peasant wars of the Middle Ages. Hundreds of thousands of Kirghiz, Kazakhs, and Uzbeks paid with their lives for that first revolt.

Neither anger nor justice, not even the slaughter of many people, was sufficient to bring this great empire down. Only when the empire was so beaten from without and so rotted from within that its peasants, its workers, its soldiers, no longer found in it either security or hope, only when the long suffering of millions had developed thinking leaders and disciplined followers, did the revolution come. Then it came swiftly, for its leaders knew how to seize the opportunity.

Great strikes of starving workers broke out in Petersburg in February, 1917. Men and women marched through the streets crying: "Peace! Land! Bread! Down with the tsar!" The tsar sent troops to suppress the demonstrators; machine guns rained bullets from roofs into the crowd.

On February 27 some soldiers refused to fire any longer at the people. The tsar heard of it at his headquarters and under advice of counselors resigned. For several months cabinets rose and fell; none proved able to ride the whirlwind that was sweeping the land. On November 7, 1917, a party known as Bolsheviks, whose leader was Nikolai Lenin, took power under the slogan "Peace, land, and bread!"

LENIN, STRATEGIST OF REVOLUTION

LENIN CAME FROM EXILE. Thousands of Russia's ablest, most progressive people were in prison or exile during the rule of the tsar. The abdication of Nikolai the Second in March, 1917, freed them to return; they came in large numbers from the jails, the salt mines, the icy wastes, and from foreign countries, bringing many and conflicting ideas on how to save and improve their native land.

Two among these thousands succeeded; their plans made history. One of them, Vladimir Ilych Ulianov, came from Switzerland; the name under which he wrote was Nikolai Lenin. A follower of his, Joseph Vissarionovich Dzhugashvili, came back from a hut in the Arctic; he was called by his comrades Stalin, Man of Steel.

LENIN

Lenin was forty-seven years old. He had spent his life studying the reasons for Russia's backwardness and why all those who had tried to reform it had failed. He had organized a political party opposed to the tsardom. He had been thrown into prison and exiled. His secretary, Nadezhda Krupskaia, joined him and married him; they spent their honeymoon amid Siberian snows. Finally they were allowed to leave Russia. They were living in Zurich, in a rented room of an old, dark house dating back to the sixteenth century. It was not comfortable; they dared open their windows only at night, for there was a little sausage factory in the house from which a frightful smell arose all day. But Lenin had been in worse places.

Lenin continued his researches in the Zurich library, wrote and smuggled his writings to his followers in Russia. He was lonely for his own people, because news came with difficulty across the World War. He tried to convince other exiles that the fall of the tsar was near; they must prepare to take part in great changes. People would not be convinced but began to avoid him. His wife thought it tragic to see "his terrific energy, his boundless devotion to the workers falling vainly to earth, his clear analysis of events quite fruitless." He seemed to her like the white polar wolf she had seen in a zoo, whose keeper had told her: "All wild animals get used in time to confinement, bears, tigers, lions. Only the white wolf from the Russian north never gets used to cages. Day and night he hurls himself against the iron bars of his prison."

Suddenly the news came that the tsar had fallen. Krupskaia told of it later. "Ilych's breathing quite stopped. He rushed here and there to learn how to get back to Russia." This was not easy during war. Finally he got a passport and gave his wife two hours to pack everything. They went across Germany in a sealed car to Sweden; thence they went through Finland to Petersburg.

"In Finnish trains we went over the border. Everything was already so dear, so homelike—those bad little third class cars with Russian soldiers. We felt tremendously happy . . . soon we came to Petersburg. The people, workers and soldiers came out to greet their leader. . . . Around us was an ocean of people like an elemental force of nature. . . . Red flags, a guard of honor of Kronstadt sailors, armored cars, a chain of working men and women guarded the road. Ilych was lifted to an armored car. He spoke a few words. Around him were those who in all the world were nearest to him, the masses of workers."

The crowd that welcomed Lenin represented one of the political parties striving to organize the chaos left by the tsar's fall. It was called the Bolshevik Party, later the Communist Party. It had a definite plan of action. Lenin's clear thinking had made him the leader.

Lenin grew up in a town on the Volga where his father was director of rural schools for the province. He heard his father's dream of educating peasants; he saw his father ride long distances on horseback, organizing schools before the railroad came. When there were 400 schools with 20,000 pupils, the Orthodox Church took them over and used them to teach obedience to the tsar. Lenin's father felt that the work of his life was wasted. Lenin's older brother was executed at the age of twenty-one, charged with a plot against the life of the tsar. The only evidence against him was that he got a friendly letter from a student who was really in such a plot.

The young Lenin learned from these two disasters. He planned, carefully and scientifically, a different way to overthrow tsardom and build the power inherent in the people—not by educating scattered peasants, not by rash acts of students, but by hard-knit organization of a working class that was appearing and increasing in Russia. This class had essential power.

Power was never an end in itself for Lenin. He saw power impersonally, disregarding his own life. He held that men must study the forces developing in human society and use them to create a better world. The tsardom was collapsing through corruption and inefficiency; the collapse should be hastened, for Russia could then swiftly become the most prosperous and progressive land on earth. The needed changes could not be made by the upper class, which profited from tsardom. The peasants were too scattered in their interests to hold a firm, continuing government through the harsh period of change; that was why peasant wars always failed. But a new class was appearing, the industrial workers. They came from the peasants and knew the peasant's needs, but their factory life made them better informed and more united than peasants. Their interest was against tsardom; they had their hands on the mighty mechanism of modern production, the base of modern power.

This working class, said Lenin, was strategic. They could be educated and organized to take power from the falling tsardom and create new government. Their government, however, would last only if it swiftly satisfied the peasants, who made up most of the people. They must rapidly develop the nation's resources through great publicly owned enterprises; they must supply electricity throughout the country. They must induce peasants to form large, cooperatively owned farms on which modern machinery could be used to best advantage. Above all, the common people everywhere must be aroused, educated, urged to criticize the public enterprises and make suggestions for betterment, and given incentive to rise to posts in industry and government.

This view of social change was not original with Lenin. It was first proposed by Karl Marx and was known as the Marxist view. Lenin contributed a new strategy, the form of the Bolshevik Party. Unlike previous parties the Bolsheviks would not take members who merely agreed with their views. They required that each member take active part in organizing some group of workers. Every member must study Russia's social problems and help organize campaigns for better wages, improved housing, or even such simple things as hot water for tea in railway stations. Thus they would learn the people's needs and also how to lead the people. Members who could not win such simple leadership were expelled as useless. Thus an active political party with wide connections of leadership was built.

When Lenin returned to Russia, April 3, 1917, the country was in chaos. Peasants were seizing nobles' land; workers were starving, factories closing for want of materials; soldiers were deserting from the front. Different cabinets claimed power but proved unable to create order. Meanwhile factory workers and regiments of soldiers were electing councils—soviets—to voice their demands. The Bolsheviks promoted these soviets and tried to get elected in them. They declared that these organizations formed a new basis for government, more democratic than any government Russia had ever had. Through these soviets even the commonest worker who could not read and write could express his grievances. The soviets, said Lenin, could therefore command the confidence of those classes most needed for national stability, the workers in production and the soldiers at the front.

In July, Lenin was hiding in a swamp on the Finnish border. He was sleeping in a haystack in hourly peril of death. He was also writing a pamphlet: *Can the Bolsheviks Keep Power?* This was a remarkable title, for so far the Bolsheviks had had no power; they could not even save their leader from execution except by hiding him in a swamp. Lenin was so sure of the future that he analyzed all the different political parties and showed how each in turn would fall. Power would then come to the Bolsheviks; Lenin analyzed their support and what tactics they must use to harness the raging torrent of popular revolt to the turbines of power to produce what the people desired. He sent this manual of tactics to his Central Committee from the swamp where he was hiding, with a price of $100,000 on his head.

In October, Lenin returned secretly to Petersburg and told his Central Committee that the time had come to take power. A Congress of Soviets would soon meet representative workers and soldiers from all the factories and battle fronts. In it the Bolsheviks would have a majority.

"Now is the time, not a week sooner or later," declared Lenin. "If we wait we shall lose the faith of the workers who have given us the majority in their soviets and expect us to use it. We must take power under the slogans: 'All power to the soviets! Land to the peasants! Bread to the hungry! Peace to the people!' "

The act of revolution was swift and simple. A call was sent out and a special committee under Stalin set up to correlate activities. Soldiers and sailors and armed workers of Petersburg seized telephone, telegraph, and government offices, and stormed the Winter Palace—from which Alexander Kerensky, then prime minister, fled. This happened in a single day, November 7, 1917.

On the same day the All-Russian Congress of Soviets of Workers' and Soldiers' Deputies, already in session, declared itself to be the government. It passed three decrees: on peace, on land, and on state power. The decree on peace proposed to all warring countries to start negotiations for a "just peace without annexations and without indemnities." The decree on land abolished the ownership of land by the nobles, the monasteries, and the tsar and made all land the nation's public property, in which all peasants tilling the soil had permanent user's rights. The decree on government transferred power to the Soviets.

Telegrams poured in from all parts of the land announcing the establishment of local soviet governments. Peasants elected village soviets and sent deputies to a Congress of Peasant Soviets, which joined with the Congress of Soviets of Workers' and Soldiers' Deputies to form a joint government. Peasants, workers, soldiers, began to take the orders of this new government. Thus began a new order and new law. The new government called itself a Soviet Republic. Lenin was chairman of the Council of People's Commissars, a post similar to prime minister. Stalin was chosen People's Commissar of Nationalities, similar to a cabinet post in charge of minor nationalities.

To take power proved easy; it was done in a day. To hold power proved harder; it took many years. The previous chiefs of government, with the nobles and heads of industry, fled to the borders and organized armies with the help of foreign governments. The German Kaiser seized Poland and the Baltic States; sent troops to Finland to set up a government under Baron Mannerheim; sent troops into the Ukraine and Caucasus to seize grain, coal, iron, and oil. Great Britain, France, Japan, and the United States of America—partly to check the Germans and partly to overthrow the Bolsheviks—sent troops to the Arctic coast at Archangel, into Siberia through Vladivostok, into the Caucasus and Central Asia.

These wars of intervention, so called because they were foreign and civil war combined, lasted until 1920–21. When they were over, Finland, Poland, Latvia, Estonia, and Lithuania had been set up as separate states; Bessarabia had been seized by

Rumania. All the rest of Russia was ruled by Congresses of Soviets.

The Russia that had collapsed from war exhaustion, under the tsar, managed to fight on under Lenin for three more years. This was partly through hope in a better future and partly because Lenin seized all food and all factories, using everything for national defense. When the last invaders were finally expelled, Russia lay prostrate without machines, raw materials, or crops. Two years of drought brought terrible famine in 1921, costing millions of lives. The American Relief Administration, which was feeding starving folk all over Europe, fed starving Russians too. This was the first move by any outsider to help the Russians. The Russians have always remembered it.

As soon as war was over, Lenin's policy of taking everything for the war—known as "war communism"—relaxed. Peasants were allowed to sell crops in open market; individuals were allowed to open small shops and factories on license from the state. The government turned its attention to the mines, transport, the steel and iron industry; these bases of economic life had been ruined most. Painfully these were rebuilt through sacrifices by their workers, who donated many Saturdays and holidays to make locomotives, streetcars, and other equipment as a gift to their commonwealth. Lenin had rightly counted on their devotion to their common properties.

Life improved, but Lenin's life was over. His last important act was the adoption of the NEP, or New Economic Policy, above described. On January 21, 1924, he died after a long and lingering illness. During bitter January frosts millions of people filed past the bier to take a last look at their leader. He was embalmed and laid in a glass coffin in a marble mausoleum below the Kremlin wall; the people still pass and see him lying lifelike with the Order of the Red Flag pinned to his breast.

The foreign world thought of him as a creator of upheaval, but the people of Russia had learned to know him as the steady preacher of hard work and discipline and punctuality and efficiency and all those unromantic virtues that became romantic when Lenin showed that they would bring Russia out of its old chaos into an order in which life would be secure. When Lenin died the standard of living of the Russian people was below even the meager standard they had known in prewar days under the tsar. Nine years of war and famine took heavy toll. But crops and factory production were on the increase—an increase in which everyone helped and whose benefits everyone shared. The people had caught Lenin's vision of a Russia which might be the world's most prosperous and progressive state.

To the peasants he was the leader who gave them, at last, their land. To city workers he was the comrade who gave them dominion over government and industry, helping each man to rise to his highest possible post. Women knew him for his challenging summons to equality: "Every kitchen maid must learn to rule the state." Children knew that he said: "What is most necessary is to study, and then to study and finally to study." Legends about him circulated among Moslem people of Central Asia celebrating him as the "Master of all knowledge who defended us from Christian cruelty."

All the people knew that he always acted as one of them, never demanding personal comfort or privilege. His two-room apartment in the Kremlin was plain even to bareness, with an oilcloth on the dining-room table, the only decorations being flowerpots on the window sills. The gifts of special food or fuel sent to him by admiring peasants he gave to the common storerooms, while he lived on the rationed diet of black bread and the meager publicly served meal. More important than this, he trusted the people with the knowledge of his difficulties and failures. In advocating the peace treaty with Germany he called it a "robber peace" to which Russia through weakness was forced; in advocating his New Economic Policy he called it a "necessary retreat." He began one New Year's telephone conversation thus: "Let us hope we make fewer mistakes this year than last."

Through this frankness Lenin aroused in tens of millions of people the knowledge that everyone's effort and sacrifice were needed and the belief that this joint effort and sacrifice would succeed. Through it he aroused trust in his government and the great energy of the people's will. It was left to others to realize his vision of a prosperous Russia; he died at the end of the most difficult years. But he left an organization that could go on without him, that depended on no single man. He himself saw clearly the greatness of Russia's future and made the initial plan.

"The dreamer in the Kremlin," he was called by H. G. Wells, the famous British writer who visited Russia in the dark days of 1920 and heard from Lenin's lips the "plan of electrification" to be achieved within fifteen years. H. G. Wells had imagined many utopias in his writings, but he could not imagine any such incredible dream as this. For Holland, for Great Britain, such wide electrification might be possible, but not for this ruined Russia. Even while the engineers worked on their mighty projects, the electric bulbs were flickering out on their tables as the few existing power plants ceased to operate. Less than ten years after Lenin's death not only his great "plan for electrification" but other plans far greater had already been achieved.

They were achieved through Stalin, who followed Lenin. But the Russian peasants call their electric lights the "lamps of Ilych."

37

STALIN, BUILDER OF THE USSR

STALIN—MAN OF STEEL came from the fragrant south, from Georgia, land of golden wine and dark-eyed women. He was born to a shoemaker father in a little town of the hills. As a lad of fourteen—his nickname then was Soso—he came upon the problem of oppressed nations when his proud father got him into the Tiflis Theological Seminary, run by Imperial Russia to control the Georgian Church. Bright Georgian boys were taught that the tsar was the head of God's Church. This would help suppress the Georgian land by religion.

Soso didn't like the doctrine. He found a forbidden book by a German Jew named Karl Marx. He read: "The philosophers have only interpreted the world; our business is to change it."

He joined the Social Democratic Labor Party, organized Tiflis railway workers into a union, and was promptly expelled from the seminary.

Young Soso, the student, vanished; he became an organizer of workers, living dangerously under many names. He was daring and energetic; he organized workers in the Caucasus and elsewhere. He led the oilworkers of Batum in a strike against the foreign Baron Rothschild; shook ancient Tiflis with a modern May Day demonstration; joined Lenin at a conference in Stockholm; edited a Bolshevik newspaper in Petersburg, the capital of the tsar. The tsar's police listed him as the "terrible Vissarionovich, who wants to change the world."

They arrested him often; they beat him up in dungeons. They banished him four times to different places in the Arctic; four times he got away. The fifth time, in 1913, they sent him to the farthest north of Asia where the great Yenesei River flows to the frozen ocean and only a handful of Eskimos are huddled against the polar night. From this place there was no escaping.

In the years before the revolution Stalin was not just a man of action. He was thinking out the problems of his people and writing articles about them. He was writing science and it was dry as dust and clear as the stars of the desert. He was working out the definition of a nation. What is a nation? How does it come to be? What rights has a nation? May it develop without limit or what should limit it? How can nations get the benefits that come through union without too greatly giving up their individuality?

These were the problems he thought about. It was natural that he should think about them, for Georgia, his country south of the Caucasus, had been for three thousand years a caldron of national wars and hates. The problems he faced have puzzled men throughout modern history; they are still the problems we all must face in building a peaceful world. Stalin knew that they were problems of deep importance on which he wanted to be very clear.

Some people were saying that a nation depends on a common blood or race. This was the theory that was later taken by the Nazis; they declared that there were "superior races" and "inferior races" and that the "superior race" had the right to conquer and enslave all the rest. This man in exile was fighting that idea in his writings. Hitler had not yet been heard of, but this man was already fighting the Hitler idea. A nation, he claimed, depends on a common culture. "A nation," he wrote, "is an historically evolved community of language, territory, economic life and psychological make-up, manifested in a community of culture." He was weighing every word carefully. Someday every one of those words would explode into billions of rubles spent for factories, schools, and theaters, into proud nations rallying for war.

What rights has a nation? Some people claimed that nations are not subject to moral law but may expand at other nations' expense. Stalin wrote that a nation "has the right to arrange its life as it sees fit without stamping on the rights of other nations." It has the right to join with other nations to secure the benefits of a joint military strength and economic wealth. It has also the right to secede from such a union.

How can nations unite without losing their individuality? This is a problem that faces us all for the rest of our days. No nation today has all the things—good soil, coal, iron, oil, and other minerals—that are needed for a prosperous life. Strength and prosperity are increased by union with other nations. But every nation wants also to be individual and free. For thousands of years conquerors have tried to unite nations by force. Stalin wrote that no union made by force is permanent. A union is stable only if the nations join voluntarily and are free to leave, and if all, whether large or small nations, are equal in rights.

Very few people read Stalin's pamphlet on nations. His fellow Bolsheviks did. He had a name among them as a hot fighter but a cool thinker. Through this and other pamphlets he became their chief expert on the problem of the relation between nations and minor nationalities. When the Bolsheviks took power in 1917 they made him Commissar of Nationalities, in charge of the many non-Russian peoples in the new state.

In 1922 Stalin became Secretary of the ruling party, which discussed all important policies before presenting them to the government. It was a highly strategic position. Discussions affecting the entire future of the Soviet government went on for several years between a group led by Leon Trotsky and the increasing majority which centered around Stalin.

Trotsky's followers believed that a backward country like Russia with little modern industry and very primitive farming could not be made into a strong state without foreign help. They wanted the Soviet government to promote revolution in other countries so that some nation like Germany, with skilled workers and modern industry, might become part of the Soviet Union and organize its inefficient workers. This policy clearly led to friction and probable war with other countries; it later led Trotsky's followers into relations with Germany which caused them to be accused of conspiracy to overthrow the USSR. A number of them were executed.

Stalin held that the people of the Soviet Union were able to build a strong and prosperous state on the base of public and cooperative enterprises. This should be their chief concern. To do this they must seek peace with other nations and avoid all interference in other nations' internal affairs. They must build modern industry and modern mechanized farming more rapidly than this had ever been done in the world before. This required good planning, great devotion, and heavy sacrifice, but the people could be aroused to this sacrifice if they understood that the very independence of the country and the existence of its Soviet government were at stake.

"Either perish or overtake the advanced countries and surpass them . . . this is how history has put the question," Lenin had said. Stalin told the chiefs of Soviet industry in the spring of 1931 that their country would be overthrown by war unless they caught up with the foremost countries of Europe within ten years. Ten years later Hitler attacked the Soviet Union with an armed force greater than the world had previously seen.

The Soviet Union was ready, for Stalin's policy won and Trotsky lost out in the discussions of 1924–1927. In the following years the Soviet Union made a swifter advance both in industry and farming and in education than had ever been seen in history.

In early 1933, at the end of the first Five Year Plan, Stalin announced that the former backward peasant Russia had become the world's second industrial country, next only to the United States. The number of industrial workers had doubled in five years from eleven to twenty-two million; industrial output had doubled. Tractors, automobiles, harvester combines, and every kind of modern machine was being produced. They were still produced very inefficiently, at tremendous waste and expense. Many American engineers, employed to organize the new industry, protested against the waste.

"We wasted and broke machines," admitted Stalin, "but we gained what is more important—time."

After the first Five Year Plan the country plunged into a second. By 1935 some of the once-inexperienced workers began

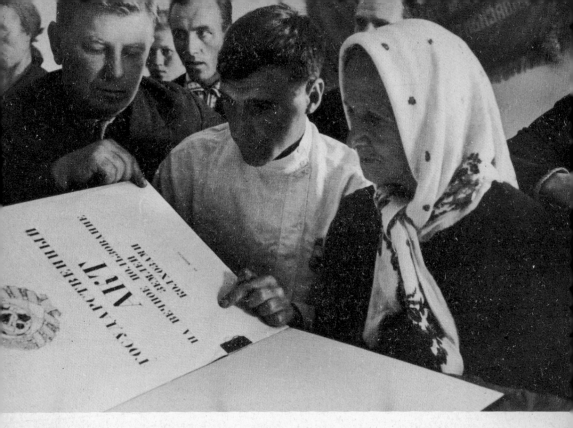

The Five Year Plan in action—farmers near Moscow study the Land Act—miners discuss new methods at the Donbas coal pits

to break world records. Some coal miners in the Donbas doubled the German standard; some forgemen in the Gorky auto works broke standards set by Ford. These were exceptional cases in a great sea of inefficiency. Everybody celebrated them; for the first time the Soviet people felt that they were no longer "backward Russians" as they had been for more than a hundred years. In every branch of industry and farming people fought for world records. The feeling of the young people was expressed by young Nina Kameneva when she broke a world's altitude record in parachute jumping and remarked on landing: "The sky of our country is the highest in the world."

Toward the end of the second Five Year Plan the country's leaders began to speak of their plans as "victorious"; the economic base of the land was secure.

"The greatest wealth of a land is people," said Stalin. Giant farms and industries are not enough; the people must be developed to manage and enjoy their natural wealth. It is simple to say: "Educate them." But education itself is not simple; it is of many kinds. What kind of education? How was it to be done?

The numerous nationalities of the USSR speaking different languages ranged from reindeer-keeping Eskimos with very little culture to ancient civilizations like the Armenian and Georgian, whose culture goes back for thousands of years. Fifty-eight of these nationalities with a total of twenty million people did not even have an alphabet, much less any books. No attempt should be made to make different nationalities resemble one another, in Stalin's view. Even the smallest and most ignorant peoples, even Eskimos and Kirghiz, have developed some form of national culture which must be respected, since it is unique and enriches the great variety of human culture. Respect for racial and national differences, for different traditions and civilizations, is part of the respect we owe to human individuality. So each national group must be encouraged to develop its own peculiar art and culture and customs, as long as these do not interfere with others.

Following this policy, Soviet scientists busied themselves developing alphabets for peoples who had none, publishing books in approximately one hundred languages, training teachers, and opening schools. Industries of modern type were started among the most backward peoples; everyone was encouraged to learn. The result was tremendous. The most spectacular progress made anywhere in the USSR was among these backward nationalities. In the Union as a whole the industrial output doubled during the first Five Year Plan; but the great plains of Kazakhstan saw a more than fourfold growth, while the Central Asian Republics multiplied their output sixfold.

Stalin's rise to power came through all these successes. He is a daring but painstaking builder; the rise of his type is slow but sure. In the early days of revolution he was hardly known outside the Bolshevik Party. Upper party circles began to speak of him as "our coming man" because of his judgment and sense of timing and of social forces; they said that "so far in the Revolution he has not once guessed wrong." Stalin became widely known outside party circles when he met with congresses of industrial leaders and workers, leading them to success in the first Five Year Plan. He was first accepted as leader by the great mass of peasants when his famous article "Dizziness from Success," March, 1930, checked the worst abuses of cooperative farming and made it plain that cooperation was voluntary and no one could be forced to join.

People who meet Stalin are first impressed by his directness and simplicity; next they notice his clearness in discussion and the skill with which he draws out everybody's best ideas and

combines them into a joint decision on which all agree. Gradually they become aware of his colossal knowledge, his keen
analysis, his grip of world politics, his willingness to face facts,
and his long view of history which fits the immediate problem
not only into the present but into the past and future too. He
believes in decisions reached through committee discussion,
rather than in individual decisions. There is, he told Emil
Ludwig, too large a percentage of error in any individual brain.

Stalin first appeared as leader of the whole Soviet people
when in 1936, as chairman of the Constitutional Commission,
he presented the present Constitution of the USSR. It was
drawn up by thirty-one of the country's ablest historians and
political scientists, who were instructed to devise the most ac-
curate machinery for obtaining the "will of the people"
through governmental forms.

In the great white hall of the Kremlin Palace 2016 delegates assembled in the congress that adopted the "Stalin Constitution," as it is known today. It was a congress of record
makers in every branch of farming, industry, and science. Here
sat Lysenko, most daring plant breeder; Burdenko, the famous
surgeon; Komarov, vice-president of the Academy of Sciences;
Moskvin, the famous actor. Here were directors of great factories: Zavenyagin, chief of Magnitogorsk Steel Works, already
the largest in Europe; Bruskin, who organized production of
caterpillar tractors at Chelyabinsk, the largest tractor factory in
the world. Among others there were 261 of the new-style farmers, all of them specialists.

This was the new Soviet Union emerging from two Five
Year Plans—a land of energetic, skilled, progressive people
priding themselves on their science, their industry, and their
farms. The Constitution itself reflected these changes. Voting
henceforth was to be not by show of hands in open meeting, as

in the first illiterate days, but by universal, direct, equal, and secret ballot for all citizens over eighteen. Equal rights for women and for all citizens irrespective of race and nationality were declared. Six articles guaranteed freedom of conscience; of worship; of speech, press, assembly, and organization.

However the Constitution may work in practice, its adoption was intended as a direct challenge to the theories and practice of Nazi fascism, which had risen to power in Berlin. Nazi Germany denounced democracy as outworn, decadent. All Soviet speakers hailed democracy; far from being decadent, they said, it had never been fully tried. While Hitler preached the view of "superior and inferior races," the Soviet Constitution made even the preaching of race privilege or inferiority a crime. Stalin directly challenged Hitler in what is perhaps the most

A sanatorium for Red Army men in the beautiful resort town of Sochi, on the Black Sea

sweeping statement ever made of equality: "Neither language nor color of skin nor cultural backwardness nor the stage of political development can justify national and race inequality."

Tens of millions of people in all the cities and villages of the USSR poured into the wintry streets with bands and banners to welcome the new Constitution of the USSR. Thenceforth the story of the USSR becomes not only the history of a federal union but the richly varied history of its many sovereign republics, each of which has its own pride.

RUSSIANS, PIONEERS OF THE NORTH

The Russian Republic—its full name is the Russian Soviet
Federated Socialist Republic, or RSFSR for short—occupies
only part of the former Russian Empire. This empire has become the USSR—a union of sixteen republics, all sovereign
and equal in rights. The Russian Republic is by far the largest,
with three-fourths of the territory and nearly two-thirds of the
population. It is 6,375,000 square miles in area—twice the size
of the United States—with more than a hundred million people.
Despite its preponderant population the Constitution of the
Union permits no federal law to be passed by Russian votes
unless the majority of the republics concur.

Russia is the guardian of the Soviet north. It includes the entire Arctic coastline, the tundra belt, and most of the great forest belt of the USSR. It possesses more than two-thirds of the grainlands and produces more than two-thirds of the industrial output. The RSFSR contains the greatest cities: Moscow, Leningrad, and many famous cities of the Volga and the Urals —among others Stalingrad.

As the strongest of the republics, Russia has given experience and skilled workers to all the others. She is the "first among equals."

The Russians are one of the world's great pioneering peoples. Their settlers crossed Siberia a century earlier and somewhat faster than American settlers crossed North America. They hopped from island to island along the Aleutians, occupied Alaska, and set outposts on the California coast in days of Spanish rule. Here they met the Americans, circling the world in the other direction. These two pioneering peoples carried Europe's civilization around the globe.

The character of the Russians was formed in subduing a continent of virgin forests and northern rivers. They show daring initiative, careful planning, personal courage, and unusual endurance. These are also qualities of the western American, the Canadian, the Australian. The Russians add a touch of philosophic detachment, a "long view" of events in relation to geography and history. Their characteristic phrase "Nichevo" means that no individual fortune matters very much.

The people of all sixteen republics speak of Moscow as the "Center." It is the capital both of the Russian Republic and of the USSR. The center of Moscow is the Kremlin, a high fortified enclosure of palaces and churches built by successive tsars. Ruby-colored stars, emblems of the USSR, gleam on its lofty pointed towers. Twelve wide boulevards branch out from the

Kremlin like spokes of a wheel. They continue through the city as its main streets, and beyond the city as highways radiating to all parts of the land.

The saying goes: "Above Moscow stands the Kremlin, above the Kremlin only the stars."

Moscow became a metropolis during the two Five Year Plans. It became the greatest railway center in Europe, with a quarter of a million passengers coming and going every day. Its eleven railways were connected by a Belt Line in the suburbs. Mrs. Zinaida Troitskaia, who got her start as the first woman locomotive engineer, became superintendent of this Belt Line, which helped make Moscow the strong fortress city of the second World War. Moscow reached more than four million population.

The Moscow subway was made the most beautiful in the world without regard to cost. "It must give an example of shining beauty because so many people see it every day," the planners said. The best architects designed the underground stations of polished marble and granite from every republic of the USSR. Artists competed to decorate them with statuary and frescoes. The subway was ventilated with more air and lighted with greater brilliance than any other in the world. It was the pride of the USSR.

Most of Moscow's population gave occasional Sundays to cart away dirt. For the first weeks after it was finished the subway was used only for "joy rides," beginning with the Supreme Soviet of the USSR and ending with workers who had done well in their factories. Farms for hundreds of miles around were allowed to send their "champions" to Moscow for a free subway ride. The trains waited at the stations for the visitors to inspect the architecture, pictures, and escalators. When all had thoroughly enjoyed their subway they used it to go to work.

Moscow is the center of Soviet culture. It has seventy higher institutions of learning. Its All-Union Lenin Library, with over ten million volumes, is one of the largest libraries in the world. Moscow has the world's largest publishing houses; it prints books in ninety-three languages. It publishes nearly three hundred newspapers, of which the two largest have circulations of several million. Moscow has nearly fifty "theaters." The Russians use this word not merely for a building but for a permanent organization of full-time actors and directors, who develop their special style of art. Festivals of art and drama come to Moscow from all sixteen republics.

The Academy of Sciences of the USSR is housed in another large cluster of buildings in a park overlooking the Moscow River. It has branches in all the republics. It centralizes the scientific knowledge of the Union in its many institutes and commissions on world resources, economics, mathematics, soil chemistry, the stratosphere, and other subjects. The roads to the North Pole and to the stratosphere start from Moscow. After the scientists have prepared the bases, the pilots take off from Moscow airfields. Scientific congresses of all kinds come to Moscow—including such world congresses as that of the world's geologists and the world's physiologists.

The Moscow River could not give enough water for this growing center, so the Moscow-Volga Canal was built. The upper waters of the Volga River are stored in a new lake 126 square miles in surface. From this "Sea of Moscow" the water is forced uphill across a low divide and then flows down into the Moscow River, which brings it by natural channel back to the middle Volga. The canal is eighty miles long with seven lake reservoirs and seven hydroelectric stations. All structures were designed not only for efficiency but to beautify the countryside. Scores of villages had to be removed; their inhabitants were given new areas with modern houses at government expense.

Moscow—the famous Red Square

The Moscow-Volga canal   The Moscow subway

Since May 2, 1937, the waters of the largest river in Europe have been flowing under the Kremlin walls, enlarging the old Moscow River fivefold. The Soviet capital is connected by navigable waterway not only with the Caspian Sea but with two oceans, the Arctic through the White Sea and the Atlantic through the Baltic. Other canals are planned which will connect Moscow with the Black Sea and the Azov, making this center of the continent a port of five seas.

The "Moscow Sea" is of use not only to Moscow. It is also a first step in controlling spring floods and in reconstructing the great Volga River throughout its length. "Mother Volga," as the Russians call the river, is not doing her duty by the Russian countryside. In former days the upper forests were wastefully logged; so the spring thaw brings great floods, which shift the channel and make sandbanks. The river becomes shallow in summer. At its lower end, after passing the city of Stalingrad, the Volga flows sluggishly below ocean level, breaking into many channels to enter the Caspian Sea. Here are large regions that might become fertile but that lack water. The Volga, uncontrolled, brings them no useful water. It passes many industrial cities but gives them no electric power.

The plans to reconstruct the Volga were made under many commissions of the Academy of Sciences. They involve even the changing of climate in a large area. The river will become a chain of great lakes, holding the spring floods and releasing them for irrigation and electric power. Since this might drop the level of the Caspian Sea and make the deserts of Turkmenia even drier, some of the full northern rivers that now fall into the Arctic will be diverted to the upper Volga—increasing its waters.

Irrigation is planned for ten million acres on the lower left bank of the river, thus moderating the dry climate. The hydroelectric stations planned include one at Samara Bend; this will be the world's largest, with a capacity of 3,400,000 kilowatts—almost twice the size of the Grand Coulee in Washington, which is now the world's largest with 1,900,000 kilowatts. Part of this cheap electricity will be transmitted west as far as Moscow and east as far as the Urals. There is a two-hour difference in sun time between Moscow and the Urals; so this wide distribution will give a more stable peak load in the evening, thus further cheapening the power.

The reconstruction of the Volga will change the life along its banks much as did the reconstruction of the Tennessee River under the famous Tennessee Valley Authority, but on a much larger scale.

The All-Union Lenin Library in Moscow which houses the largest collection of volumes in the USSR

In the days when Hitler's armies were assaulting the gates of Moscow many writers assumed that if the "Center" were taken the land would fall to pieces. The Soviet people knew that even if they lost all of European Russia they had a great inland fortress behind the Urals that could produce food, clothing, and weapons for a last-ditch defense.

This fortress is a self-sufficient inland empire, larger than all of western Europe. It is protected from invasion and even from bombing by two thousand miles of Russian land. It possesses coal, iron, wheat, and timber. The area was developed from 1930 onward on Stalin's initiative. When Japan invaded Manchuria in 1931, apparently undecided whether next to attack China or the USSR, the building of this fortress was speeded by sacrificing other parts of the Five Year Plan. It became a base in the very heart of the USSR, producing all the war necessities from tanks and munitions to canned meat, powdered milk, and wheat. Its streams of supplies can be sent easily in any direction either to the west or to the south or east.

The western citadel of this fortress is Magnet Mountain (Magnitogorsk) in the southern Urals. Its single mountain of high-grade iron ore is enough to supply even a modern war for a generation. The eastern citadel is Kuznetsk Basin, with 450 billion tons of coal. The thousand odd miles between the two citadels are filled by the grainfields of western Siberia and by inexhaustible timber reserves.

Many industrial cities grew up in the inland fortress within ten years. While the industries of central Russia increased by 87 per cent during the first Five Year Plan, the industries in this inland area increased by 285 per cent in those five years. Some of the industrial plants claim to be the largest in the world. Uralmash claims to be the world's largest heavy-machine-building plant. Chelyabinsk tractor plant was the world's largest producer of caterpillar tractors; it is making tanks today.

When Hitler invaded the USSR the inland fortress was ready to absorb the factories brought here from Leningrad and the Ukraine. Some of these were so large that it took seven thousand flatcars to transport a single great industrial plant. But the inland empire was ready; its power plants and industries had been so planned that they could at once link up new factories.

To Russian young people the Soviet Far East presents the same challenge of vast, rich, but undeveloped territory that the Far West presented to American youth fifty years ago. It calls the young, the energetic, the pioneers. In size it is comparable to northwest America from Oregon through Canada and Alaska. Vladivostok, its southern port, lies in the latitude of the northern California border. Its Arctic coast runs farther north than any part of the North American continent. The territory between contains great mountain chains, heavily wooded, full of minerals and traversed by great rivers, like the northwestern lands of America. It has gold fields opposite those of Alaska; they are as far away from the Trans-Siberian Railway as the Klondike is from the northern railways of the United States.

The Russians reached this area in the seventeenth century only a few decades after the Pilgrim Fathers landed on Plymouth Rock. Under the tsars it became the place to which lawbreakers and people who opposed the tsar were exiled. The Soviet government launched a drive to develop the Far East. The campaign became especially strong after the Japanese invaded Manchuria. A Russian population was needed to hold the Soviet Far East against Japan.

One famous city was built entirely by young people. It was called Komsomolsk, which means roughly the "City of Youth."

In 1932 the Russians decided that they needed a shipbuilding port on the Pacific farther north than Vladivostok, which is easy to bomb. Young people in all the cities and rural districts were invited to volunteer. Only those with good records were taken. It became an honor to be accepted for the "City of Youth."

The first settlers sailed for hours down the wide Amur River among virgin forests, seeing thousands of birds but no sign of man. They landed in the woods, at a spot without buildings where the surface of the eternally frozen subsoil was beginning to thaw. A veteran guerrilla of the days of Japanese intervention met them.

"Line up. This group fells trees; this group digs ditches."

"But we are skilled machinists, tool and die makers."

"That's needed later," he said.

They slept in tents marked with the names of all the Russian cities from which they came. They attacked the woods and fought mosquitoes. They pulled logs with ropes, having no horses. Then they found fifty wild horses; surrounded them, lassoed them, and made them work. After the last boat had left they lived on bear meat; there were plenty of bears in the woods. When the Amur froze they broke a canal in the ice and floated logs down it. Soon a regular sawmill whistle awoke them all in the morning. They worked when mercury in the thermometer froze.

The town grew fast in a rough-and-ready fashion. It remained a city of young pioneers. Shortly before the second World War a group of several hundred settlers came in on the last autumn boat. They brought sewing machines, trunks, children's cradles. A reception committee took them to a big grove of birch trees and said: "Here's where you will live." They were startled but not for long. The children were bundled off

The fishermen of Kamchatka, the mechanics of the Gorky auto works,
the steel workers at Magnitogorsk, are all citizens of the RSFSR

to the city day nurseries, bathed, and put to bed between white sheets. The adults began building with the help of two gangs of expert carpenters.

Ten days later there was a new settlement on the edge of the city, with paths leading through the birches from house to house. Not all the windows and doors were attached, but most of the families had already moved in. Four hundred little columns of smoke rose from homes of raw lumber where coats already hung on the walls, babies were rocking in cradles, and young housewives were taking from their trunks the table linen brought from five thousand miles away.

Several million Jews were crowded in Moldavia. Thousands of them were handicraftsmen who had little chance to develop their talents where they lived. They asked for a territory of their own in the Far East. They were given Birobidjan, an area larger than Holland located on the Trans-Siberian Railway and served by three navigable rivers. They were asked to produce furniture, carts, and consumer goods for the Far East. They tested local materials, made sample products, and at once got big orders from the growing eastern cities.

One group of furniture makers fashioned with much difficulty twelve bentwood chairs in an open-air workshop. They sent them to Khabarovsk, the capital of the Far East. They were stunned when they got a return order for "five thousand chairs immediately." With the order came money to build a factory.

All Far Eastern settlers are conscious of the threat of Japan. In case of need the Soviet Far East has its own Far Eastern Army, largely equipped from Siberia. It has also a cool-thinking pioneer citizenry who have studied modern self-defense.

Petersburg, the old capital, was built by Peter the Great as a "window on Europe." It is now called Leningrad and is the largest port and second largest city of the USSR, with nearly 3,000,000 people. Leningrad rivals Moscow with its great public library of 10,000,000 volumes; its 60 higher institutions of learning; its 142 scientific institutes, one of which is Pavlovo—an entire suburban settlement built for the work of the physiologist Pavlov. Leningrad has an older industrial tradition than Moscow. During the Five Year Plans its skilled workers were "rationed out" to start industries all over the land.

Leningrad is no longer a capital or a "window on Europe." It is a window on a great Arctic empire of which Peter the Great had only begun to dream. Today the Arctic is one of the most thrilling interests of Russian youth.

The map of the Arctic was a chain of blank spots. Russian traders went to it by river and brought furs from the native tribes. The peoples of the north lived in tents of reindeer skin in summer and in igloos of snow in winter. They had not reached the age of metal; they used stone arrowheads. They were dying out, from the hardships and from the alcohol brought by traders. Some of these native folk were exhibited in cages in a Petersburg exposition in tsarist days.

Modern Russians decided to develop their Arctic empire. Its weather affects the climate of the entire USSR, for the Arctic is the "kitchen where weather is brewed." The Arctic has resources of furs, fish, minerals, which the Russians planned to use. Besides, they wanted a waterway to connect the east and the west of their land. The Arctic Ocean was their only waterway and the only outlet for the long Siberian rivers.

The conquest of the Arctic was planned by a whole group of scientific commissions and launched from Leningrad under Professor Otto Schmidt as commander in chief. Scientific stations for weather reports were set up one by one along the Arctic coast. Trading expeditions approached from the east and from the west, going a little farther each year. Especially adapted airplanes were built for Arctic exploration.

The Committee of the North also cultivated the northern peoples. An educational institution was set up in Leningrad to study them; it listed twenty-six "nations" of the north, some of which had only a few hundred families. Alphabets were created for these peoples; books were prepared. Schools for the native peoples pushed their way along the Arctic coast, some traveling with the reindeer herds of the nomads, others building dormitories where native children spent the winter. The old trading system that had ruined the northern folk was replaced by hunters' cooperatives. Young people of the northern tribes were brought to Leningrad and trained to become executives in the Arctic. Soon the peoples of the Arctic were electing their representatives to the Supreme Soviet in Moscow. The representative from Chukotka was born in a tent of reindeer skin.

The Russians then prepared to sail from ocean to ocean across the northern coast of Asia in a single summer. The icebreaker *Sibiriakov* was the first to accomplish this, in the summer of 1932. Its screw was smashed by an ice floe; but the ship continued with sails and succeeded in reaching the Pacific, where it limped into port for repairs. A year later the *Chelyushkin* made the voyage from Europe to the Bering Strait but was caught by ice, carried back into the Arctic, and crushed there. Its crew and passengers—includirg Professor Schmidt, who was ill from exposure—were rescued by daring Soviet airmen helped by Americans from Alaska.

After two years more of preparations a regular Arctic line was established in 1935; by 1937 it carried 275,000 tons of freight. It is helped by powerful icebreakers, by lighthouses and fuel bases. Fifty-seven scientific stations are dotted along the Arctic coast, with continuous radio service. Siberian rivers have been explored that formerly had not even names. Fifteen hundred valuable mineral deposits have been found.

In summer the Arctic stations are connected by airplane as well as by steamer. These air routes began with 500 flying hours in 1932. In 1937 they flew 16,000 hours and carried 8800 passengers and 1600 tons of freight. A transpolar theater visits the Arctic settlements, playing Shakespeare and other classics for isolated stations and ships among the ice floes. In three years this theater traveled 3100 miles and gave 269 performances.

A new Arctic area grew up, consisting of scientific stations, ports, towns, and developing northern peoples. But the transport of food to this region cost several times as much as the food itself. Fresh milk and vegetables were especially needed to prevent scurvy, that scourge of the north. A special department of "polar farms" was created. A chain of experimental farms was set up along the latitude of 67 degrees, north of the Arctic Circle.

The task seemed inhumanly hard, for the ground was swampy and stony. The polar winter lasts eight months; in July the ice was still firm under the mossy hillocks. People set to work, drained the swamps, cleared them of stones, added fertilizer, developed quick-ripening varieties of seed. Tney made use of the "vernalization" method, which the Ukrainian plant specialist Lysenko was using to obtain early harvests before the southern drought. This enabled them to get harvests in the short polar summer, whose lack of heat is somewhat compensated for by its excess of light. This light, however, raises new problems; plants tend to produce leaves instead of fruit.

Potatoes, carrots, turnips, and other vegetables are now successfully raised beyond the Arctic Circle, and also a fodder grass that gives two cuttings of hay. Flowers are grown, including pinks, asters, and irises. Through the long polar night the plants are kept alive in electrically lighted greenhouses. Vegetables and mushrooms ripen under glass in April at Dixon Bay, which is farther north than any spot on the American continent.

Life on the Arctic coast was not enough for the Russians. They decided to set up a camp on the ice at the North Pole and see what happened to it. Many important scientific facts could thus be learned.

The summer of 1937 is famous in polar history. In that year two Russian pilots, Chkalov and Gromov, made successive flights across the North Pole to land in the United States. In the same year the floating polar station was set up on the drift ice at the North Pole. This station kept the pilots supplied with weather reports.

Preparations for the North Pole camp took more than a year. The lives of four men would depend on the accuracy of their scientific observations and the condition of their radio. Unless they could send their exact location they could never be found and taken off. They needed heavy equipment. Yet all equipment and food for four men for a year must be kept within ten tons. Ordinary canned food was far too heavy. Special methods of extreme dehydration had to be found. All equipment had to be made to order, to combine lightness with strength.

On May 21, 1937, a four-motored orange-colored plane landed at the pole on the drifting ice. A few days later three other planes arrived. The first scientific discovery was made: it was possible to land near the pole, a fact that had been disputed before. Two weeks later the planes took off, leaving four men behind.

These four men—their leader was Ivan Papanin—began backbreaking work. It was hard enough to exist. All summer the ice was covered with lakes of melting snow; they had to keep

Horsemen watering their herd on the steppes near Kuibyshev

An Arctic agricultural station   *An expedition in the Altai Mountains*

moving the tent to stay out of the lakes. In winter everything was buried under drifts and had to be shoveled out regularly. The dehydrated soup they had brought took only five minutes to cook, but it required three hours, first, to bring the water to a boil.

Besides keeping alive these men had a job to do. They took sun observations to measure their drift. They took soundings to learn the ocean depth. They brought up water in a dense silken net and tested it for forms of life. They studied winds, water currents, and all the life of the polar seas. They sent and received three thousand radio messages so that their fellow scientists might have their discoveries, even if they themselves did not come back.

These four were the first to know the depth of the polar ocean. It is 14,075 feet. They were the first to know of the warm current that exists a thousand feet under the ice—the Gulf Stream from the Atlantic continuing as far as the pole. Formerly many people believed that no life could exist under the ice because it would be dark there and life needs light. These four men found that the sun penetrates sixty-six feet through ice—giving life to seaweed, which provides food for small creatures. These creatures are eaten by fish that are eaten by seals, which are eaten in turn by polar bears. This is the cycle of polar life.

They found—and this was important for their own existence —that they were not drifting around and around the pole in circles, as polar currents were assumed to flow, but were headed fast for Greenland and the southern seas. A vicious storm smote them on January 26 and continued six days. Then came jerks and cracking of ice. With thin flashlights in the polar night the men saw black water yawning beside their storage tent. Their floating cake was reduced to 100 by 150 feet.

They radioed this to Moscow and kept on with their observations.

On February 19 at 3:55 in the afternoon Radio Operator Krenkel sent direct to Stalin the last radio message of the "North Pole Drifting Observatory." Then the station closed down and the four men went on board the icebreakers that had come to them from Russia and found them near the Greenland coast. All over the USSR more than a million people breathed relief.

The North Pole campers had a triumphal entry into Moscow in autos garlanded with flowers. They were the latest heirs of a great tradition. The Russian pioneers of the virgin woods and the long rivers had made the Arctic their channel from Atlantic to Pacific and had dared the currents of the northern pole.

UKRAINIANS, SLAVS OF THE SOUTHLAND

To ALL SLAV PEOPLE the Ukraine is the beloved southland where the sun shines on the open prairie, where, in the words of Tolstoy, "the rivers flow brighter than silver, where the gentle wind rustles the tall grasses and the farm buildings are lost in cherry groves." It is the land whence the dark woodlands of northern Russia receive the spring.

The passengers on the night train south from Moscow in the first week of any May will have rubber overshoes on their feet and fur coats on their shoulders. They are leaving a gray, chilly city dripping with first thaw. When they wake in the morning the sun will be warm on tender shoots of grain and grasses. Little white houses with straw-thatched roofs nestle by the ponds. Flowering fruit trees stand like ballet girls dancing in a white and pink fairy world of perfume and light.

This is the Ukraine, bringing the springtime.

In the summer the fields are heavy with harvest. The Ukraine contains the greater part of the "black-earth area," so fertile that it produced crops even when stirred by primitive wooden plows. In former days it was known as the "Breadbasket of Europe." Under Soviet rule it became also the sugarbox of the USSR, producing two-thirds of the country's sugar beets as well as a quarter of its wheat. Its farming is richly diversified, like that of Iowa and Missouri, including corn and hogs, tobacco, fruit, grapes, oats, and potatoes.

The Ukraine is also a center of coal and iron. Its Donets Basin is the Pittsburgh valley of the USSR, with an estimated coal reserve of ninety billion tons. The famous Dnieper Dam, the "electric heart of the Ukraine," was—until destroyed in the war—one of the world's largest dams, producing more power than all the electric stations of tsarist Russia combined. The Ukraine produced three-fifths of the pig iron of the USSR, half of its coal, one-fifth of its machinery and chemical products, and one-third of its railway freight. It thus combined a well-developed agriculture with a well-developed industry.

With some 200,000 square miles of area and some forty million population (in 1941) the Ukraine is nearly as large as Iowa, Missouri, Illinois, and Indiana combined and has more than twice as many people. It lies just north of the Black Sea and just east of Poland and Rumania. In population and economic power it is the second among the Soviet Republics, the Russian Republic being first.

The Ukrainians are the second largest of the Slav groups in the USSR and have a long, proud history. In past centuries their aspirations to an independent nation of their own were never realized for they were without natural protective frontiers between the Poles and the Russians. Finally in 1917, following the revolution the Ukraine declared its independence as a Soviet Republic, and five years later became one of the four Soviet Republics which united to form the USSR.

Part of the lure that the Ukraine has for all Slavs comes from its early history. Its prairies were the old highway of the nations; great burial mounds are still found on the prairie containing prehistoric weapons and implements of tribes that migrated into Europe before the days of Greece and Rome. Here lay the outposts of the early Greeks against the Scythians. Here lay the land route of early Europe to fabled India and China. Here Marco Polo came.

Here also were the springs of Russian culture. Kiev-Russ on the Dnieper was the first Russian state. Through "Holy Kiev, mother of Russian cities," the Christian religion and the old Greek civilization came to the savage north. Early Kiev did not attempt to settle the prairies; it lay just north of them in the shelter of woods. The grasslands were held by roving horsemen who, under the leadership of Genghiz, destroyed Kiev in A.D. 1240.

Most of all, the Ukraine meant the lure of frontier freedom. When serfdom grew heavy in the north, the serf peasants fled southward to the open prairies. Thence came the name "the Ukraine," meaning "the frontier." A new type of farmer developed, the frontiersman, who plowed with a gun on his shoulder and a sword at his side. These farmers intermarried with the roving tribes, making common cause against the northern nobles.

From this intermarriage and the frontier life came Ukrainians, taller, more graceful, browner of skin and hair, than the northern Russians. Their customs were freer. Their women were sometimes independent heads of families who even,

Young Ukrainian farmers gathering to sing and dance

Korolenko Street in Kiev   A coke plant in the Donbas

though rarely, achieved divorce. Young people of the frontier chose their own mates; romantic love became the theme of ballads.

The most famous Ukrainian stronghold in the Middle Ages was the "Camp below the Rapids," some three hundred miles down-river from Kiev. (This stronghold has become the industrial town of Zaporozhie today.) Here sixty miles of rapids stopped navigation, forcing the rivermen to drag their boats a long distance overland. This was the place the early horsemen usually chose to attack the river merchants. Here were high cliffs, easily fortified. Escaped serfs from both Russia and Poland set up this "Camp below the Rapids" which chose its own "hetman," or chief, and which was strong enough to fight the Turks, the Poles, and the Russian tsar.

The Polish nobles were the most ruthless and the most hated by the Ukrainians, since they persecuted the Ukrainian form of religion. In 1648 a war of the Ukrainians broke out against the Polish nobles. The hard-pressed Ukrainian hetman called on the Moscow tsar for aid. A treaty was made by which the Ukraine became part of the rising Russian Empire, retaining certain autonomous rights. The autonomy was lost in 1783 under Catherine. She bestowed most of the rich lands on her favorites and named the territory "Little Russia," since she disliked the old free name "the Ukraine."

This beautiful fertile land has been greatly coveted. The Poles fought the Russians for it at various times for six hundred years. The Germans also wanted it for their "living space." German armies seized it in 1918 after the Russian Revolution. Most of the Ukraine changed hands ten to fifteen times during the wars of intervention. The Poles conquered Kiev in 1920. Finally the Ukrainians set up a Soviet Republic which, by the 1924 Constitution, became a sovereign state of the USSR.

After this both farming and industry rapidly developed.

Ukrainian peasants—and peasants of the USSR generally—never had individual family farms such as we know in America. They lived in villages, as they had lived in the Middle Ages when they were serfs on the lords' estates. When serfdom was abolished in 1861 many peasant families were unable to buy land at the price the landlord wanted. They remained landless farm hands, working for the landowners. Other peasants bought land; but their acreage was small and scattered in many places, so that they spent more time walking to their bits of land than in actual work on the soil.

The 1917 revolution made all land the property of the state but gave its use to the peasants. They divided it through village committees, giving to each family in proportion to the mouths it fed. The peasants found it hard to work this land even after they got it. Nobody had modern implements, fertilizer, or selected seed.

The new Soviet government encouraged peasants to form cooperative farms by putting all their scattered bits of land together and using their draft animals in common. For such farms the government reduced taxes and sold farm machinery on credit. By 1933 this form of cooperative farming became the dominant type of farming in the USSR.

All such cooperative farms get their tractors and farm machinery from a central service station known as a "Machine and Tractor Station." This was a Ukrainian invention. The first of them appeared on the prairie near Odessa in 1930. The farmers were all in desperate need of machinery, which they were unable to buy and incompetent to use. An experimental farm of the Department of Agriculture set up a machine shop with 200 tractors and the necessary implements and rented these to farms, taking its pay in crops. This center supplied tractors for 150,000 acres. Tractors worked night and day, with two or three tractor drivers for each machine.

This Tractor Station became a natural center for farm improvement. It gave winter courses for farmers and supplied farm experts to give advice. It became the agent through which the government issued farm credits. By the end of the first year the station near Odessa was buying selected seed, young apple trees, French vines, pure-bred cows, sheep, pigs, and chickens for sixty-seven villages. This organization was rapidly copied throughout the USSR. This system gives the farmers the latest machinery operated by experts and costing only rental charge. It also gets maximum use of machinery and gives the government an income in grain in return for machines.

Ukrainian farmers are no longer illiterate peasants. They buy quantities of books and subscribe to newspapers and magazines. Cooperative farms have their own "Laboratory Cottages," which connect with the experimental work of the Department of Agriculture. Villages have their own theaters and motion-picture houses, their choruses and bands. They have sport clubs where young folks learn parachute jumping, gliding, and even aviation, as well as more usual sports. Many Ukrainian farms possessed their own airplane and used it to good advantage for their guerrilla fighters when Hitler attacked the USSR.

The Ukraine is also a center of big industry. It was an important industrial district in the days of the tsar. Under Soviet rule it developed much more rapidly. Coal output reached three times that of 1913. The Donets coal basin, known as the "Donbas," became a center of throbbing, pounding activity, of hoisting towers and enormous black slag heaps, of blast furnaces roaring into the heavens, of chemical plants and steelworks with thousands of tall chimneys against a sooty sky. The found-

Machine and tractor stations service the great grain fields of the Ukraine—mechanized farming steps up the output

ries of the Ukraine claimed a steel production equal to that of Italy, Japan, and Poland together.

The hydroelectric plant built at the dam was the largest in Europe. The Dnieper Dam had a capacity of 558,000 kilowatts. Its power was cheap, costing a tenth of a cent per kilowatt-hour. Some of it went to cooperative farms for electric plowing and electric milking. Most of it went to huge industrial enterprises making aluminum and high-grade steels. A quarter of a billion dollars' worth of industrial buildings and machinery surrounded the Dnieper Dam in 1941 when Hitler entered the Ukraine. All this was dismantled or blown up to keep it from falling into the hands of the Nazis.

The Dnieper Dam was only the first step in a plan to reconstruct the entire length of the Dnieper River. It is the third largest river in Europe, being surpassed only by the Volga and the Danube. It rises in the swamps of White Russia, where peasants suffer from a surplus of water. It empties into the Black Sea through prairies that suffer from drought. The plan is to drain 2,000,000 acres of the upper swamps and use the surplus water to irrigate 8,000,000 acres near the river's mouth. The full reconstruction of the river will also connect it by canals with several other rivers, making a network of waterways across all of European Russia from the Baltic to the White Sea, the Caspian, the Black Sea, and the Azov, as Peter the Great dreamed.

The Ukraine has many great cities. Kiev, its capital, was one of the beautiful cities of the world, standing high above a great bend of the Dnieper River, with broad avenues, green parks, cathedrals with golden domes, and many institutions of learning. Odessa, the Ukrainian seaport, was founded centuries ago by Greek merchants and named for Odysseus (Ulysses). Kharkov—the Chicago of the USSR—was a great grain center and also the outlet for the Donets Basin's coal and steel. Its population of 800,000 made tractors, locomotives, and electrical equipment in giant industrial plants. Kharkov was also an important university center, with 32,000 students and 2200 scientific workers. It claimed as many college students as all of England.

All these great cities and farms were destroyed by Hitler's invasion. The German armies swept into the Ukraine in 1941. The open prairies offered no natural resistance to the rolling tanks. For more than two years the Germans held the Ukraine. German settlers and factory managers poured into the country close behind their armies; they came to take over the Ukrainian farms and factories and use this great wealth to feed their conquest of the Caucasus, Persia, India, the world.

They held the Ukraine, but most of the fabulous Ukrainian wealth escaped them. As the Germans entered, the Ukrainian farmers and factory workers destroyed the farms and took the factories away. They turned over their food products to the Red Army; they drove their tractors and trucks a thousand miles eastward to work on other Soviet farms The factory workers similarly loaded their industrial equipment on trains and sent it eastward, accompanying it in boxcars. What they could not take they destroyed, so that the Nazis might not use it for other conquests.

Here is what happened in one Ukrainian village as the Nazis approached. The young people loaded nine trucks with grain and sent them to the railway station. Four tons of barley that could not be moved were burned. The tractors plowed under the beets and then drove off with the army. The milkmaids drove the cows through the ripening grain; they were followed by eighty girls, with sickles, who chopped up what was left. The mechanics broke the fuel tank; the blacksmith destroyed the harvesters and thresher, after burying the smaller important parts. The people burned the pigsty, cowsheds, granary, beehives, and new stable. The pigs were given to the Red Army commissary. The best horses were driven to the forest for the use of the guerrillas. Even the children helped fill the village wells with earth and destroy the fishpond by breaking the dike. After this the children were sent eastward by train, while the young people took to the woods.

The first signal to the world of the Soviet people's grim determination was the blowing up of the great Dnieper Dam, and the quarter of a billion dollars' worth of industry surrounding it, in August of 1941. This was a sample of what occurred throughout the Ukraine.

The German conquerors left an even greater destruction, of a different kind. The Ukrainian people destroyed wealth that might strengthen an enemy in battle. The Germans destroyed dwellings, cathedrals, all the historical monuments of the people. When the Red Army returned, it found 40,000 corpses of persons who were thrown down a mine shaft in the Donbas and 100,000 corpses of persons slaughtered in a ravine near Kiev. The famous Kiev churches, the Holy of Holies of the early Russian Church, had been destroyed.

But the Ukrainian earth remains.

No vandal could burn it, dynamite it, poison or machine-gun it. No robber could carry it away. The fertile soil remains, and the coal and iron beneath it remain. The Dnieper River remains, flowing from the heart of the continent.

The spirit of the Ukraine remains. Even while the young men were in the Red Army driving westward, the women of the Ukraine began picking up the bricks and old iron of ruined cities; the old men and young folks began coming back with tractors to turn the fertile soil.

The Ukraine did not wait for the end of war to begin its reconstruction. As soon as the soil was free the people began to make new farms and cities better than before.

MOLDAVIA, A NEGLECTED GARDEN

IT IS SPRING in Moldavia. Once more the buds burst white and pink on apple and apricot trees. Once again the Dniester River swells with the melting snows of the Carpathian Mountains, surges between high banks and floods into morasses, and so comes south to the Black Sea.

This time the first spring thunder merges with the thunder of artillery. For it is spring of 1944. The Red Army surges westward like a river in flood, washing away the invaders. Behind the Red Army lie the liberated fields of the southern Ukraine, now deep in spring mud. Stuck in the mud are German tanks of all kinds—Tigers, Panthers, Ferdinands—passenger cars and trucks, even valises, overcoats, and boots abandoned by

79

the Germans in their disorderly flight towards the border.

Here also, through Moldavia, the Germans retreated hastily. The German colonists who had seized flour mills and oil presses, forcing the natives to bow low to the "superior race," skipped out just ahead of their army. Only beyond the river Pruth, in Rumania, did the Germans make a stiff stand. There for many weeks they held the narrow gap where the Carpathians swing closest to the Black Sea, the passage from the Russian plain to the Danube valley.

Soviet Moldavia lies between the Ukraine and Rumania. The Carpathian Mountains bound it on the north, while its southern shores are washed by the Black Sea. It is 13,600 square miles in area, half again as large as Holland, and has some 2,200,000 people. It is a garden land of rich black soil. But for centuries it has been a neglected garden. Only a small part of Moldavia has been in the USSR for any length of time. Most of it was annexed in 1940 when the territory called Bessarabia was returned by Rumania to Russia. Bessarabia forms about five-sixths of Soviet Moldavia.

In Soviet Moldavia, now that the Nazis have gone, the village elders in the shabby clay villages bring out the ceremonial tray of bread, salt, and wine, the traditional peasant welcome, and offer it to the Red Army. Dark Moldavian women present earthen pitchers of cold well water to the thirsty troops. Barefoot boys in brown homespun and tall sheepskin caps crowd around the Red Army planes on sodden fields, their brown eyes staring as if a miracle had come.

Moldavia lies at the gap between the Black Sea and the Carpathians, through which in ancient days the tribes from Asia migrated into Europe. This territory was conquered by all the tribes that passed; if they failed to conquer it, they did not get through. The gap was narrow and the tribes were many. So the population became very mixed. Some say that Moldavians are largely Slav, others that they are largely a Romanized people from Thrace.

The early Greeks knew this territory as the stronghold of the dreaded Cimmerians. Later there were Scythians here. When Trajan conquered the territory, making it part of the Roman province of Dacia in A.D. 106, the tribes of the area were Slavs. The Slavs built cities in the sixth century, some of which still exist. They joined Kiev-Russ in the great campaign against Constantinople in the tenth century. When Kiev-Russ split into principalities, one of the largest and richest was located in this area. It was called Chervonaya-Russ—Red, or Golden, Russ.

A Romanized tribe from Thrace known as Vlachs came north in the thirteenth century and drove the Slavs from part of the land. Almost at once the great Mongol invasion overwhelmed both Slavs and Vlachs in a common slavery. In the sixteenth century the Turks seized the area and the hapless land became the battleground for many successive wars between the Turks and the Poles. During this period it became known as the principality of Moldavia.

The boundaries of this medieval Moldavia changed often. On the whole it was considerably larger than Soviet Moldavia is today. It included much of what is now Rumania. In those days there was no Rumania. There was only a large territory of peasants, over which the Turks fought with the Poles and later with the Russians. The peasants developed a spoken language known as Moldavian. They had no written language. The language of the Church and of any literature that existed was the old Slavonic tongue, written down by Christian monks for Kiev-Russ.

In 1711 the feudal lord of Moldavia, seeking protection against the Turks, made a treaty with Peter the Great whereby

Moldavia became a vassal state of the Russian Empire. The Russians then fought the Turks for its possession. Moldavia changed hands five times in the next hundred years. In 1812 it was divided. Russia got the territory east of the Pruth River—known as Bessarabia—while the Turks held the Moldavian lands west of the Pruth.

Forty years later the western part of Moldavia, still under Turkish rule, joined with another subject state to form Rumania, a vassal state of the Turkish Empire. In 1877 Rumania helped Russia against the Turks and thereby won independence. The new Rumanian state wanted Bessarabia too. But the same conference of European powers that recognized Rumania as an independent state recognized Russia's right to Bessarabia.

The Rumanian rulers did not give up hopes of getting Bessarabia. They waited for their chance. After the Russian Revolution of 1917, when the troops of the German Kaiser seized the Ukraine, Rumania sent troops into Bessarabia as a "temporary measure to restore order." Rumania signed an agreement with Soviet Russia on March 5, 1918, promising to withdraw her troops within two months. Twenty-two years went by and the Rumanian troops were still there. Great Britain and France recognized Rumania's possession of Bessarabia as part of their "barbed-wire" policy against the USSR. The United States of America never recognized Rumania's right to the territory. The USSR constantly protested the seizure of Bessarabia but did not make it a cause of war. So the Rumanian troops held the territory for twenty-two years.

Nobody has ever claimed that Rumania was a modern, progressive state. But if any progress came to Rumania, none of it was allowed to reach Bessarabia while it was under Rumanian rule. Rumania was never sure how long she would be able to hold that territory. So why should she invest in improvements there? Bessarabia became the neglected garden of the Rumanian state. Rumania used it chiefly as a military outpost against the USSR.

Not a mile of new railway was built there, not a factory or hospital. The old railway network had been based on Russia as a market and Odessa as a port. These lines were cut; even the bridge across the Dniester was removed. Profitable freight was replaced by movements of troops. Trains running through Bessarabia had their windows whitewashed, and police in the corridors prevented the opening of windows. Thus the condition of Bessarabia was concealed from the world.

The peasants of Bessarabia hated their Rumanian rulers so bitterly that 153 uprisings took place in the first six years of Rumanian rule. Thirty thousand persons were killed in these uprisings. Three hundred thousand fled the country.

In 1935 the railway bridge was finally rebuilt across the Dniester by agreement between Rumania and the USSR. The USSR proposed to build the entire bridge, but Rumania refused. So the bridge was built half and half. The Soviet half was a solid structure of steel and concrete with decorative metal columns holding bright electric lights. The Rumanian half was built on wooden dikes filled with rocks; it had a rough-hewn wooden railing and was lighted by tin lanterns swinging from unpainted wooden posts.

Every new sentry who came to that bridge from the Soviet side could not suppress a grin at the contrast. What people thought on the other side of the river was hidden, because of the Rumanian police. The police would not let people from Bessarabia cross the border to see what was happening on the Soviet side. But they could not entirely conceal it, for the peasants in Bessarabia could look across the river and see new pumping stations reclaiming lands and new power plants light-

Harvesting an abundant fruit crop in Moldavia

ing villages. After a while they could see red-tiled roofs appear on peasant cottages, and even tractors in the fields.

Over there, they knew, lived their own Moldavian people, who had become part of the USSR.

A tiny piece of land inhabited by Moldavians lay on the upper Dniester in the Soviet Ukraine. It was only 3250 square miles in size, less than a sixty-mile square. It was not large enough to become a sovereign state, so it was made an "autonomous republic" under the Ukrainian Soviet Republic. Its people began to improve their land.

These Moldavians were, at the beginning, among the most ignorant folk in the USSR. They had not even a written language or an alphabet. Their only art was expressed in folk songs and in gay hand-woven rugs hung on the whitewashed walls of their cottages. Their farming was very primitive.

The chief problem of all the farmers in this sixty-mile-square Moldavia was that they had too much water in one place and too little in another. Every spring the melting snows from the Carpathians made the Dniester rise in flood. This created marshes in the lowlands along the river. The riverbanks were high, receding in wide terraces. The upper areas suffered from drought.

Sixty-mile-square Moldavia began to fight its floods and drought. The farmers organized cooperative farms and got machinery and credits from the government. They built 120 miles of earthen dikes to control the floods. They installed great pumping stations that drained water from the marshes, lifting it to irrigate the arid lands above.

Soviet Moldavia became a garden land of orchards and vineyards. It had the biggest fruit cannery in the USSR, producing 50,000,000 cans of fruit a year. Industry also developed. Be-

The men and women of Cernauti, Moldavia, gather around as the first Soviet newspaper arrives in their town

fore the Russian Revolution there were only 24 small handicraft enterprises in this small area, employing 640 workers. By 1939 there were 200 enterprises with more than 10,000 workers.

Moldavians, who formerly had no written language, now had 150 schools teaching in the Moldavian tongue. They had their own national theater, choral society, and symphony orchestra. It was all in that sixty-mile square.

The Moldavians in Bessarabia still lived without schools or tractors on the other side of the Dniester under Rumanian rule.

In the summer of 1940, when Hitler was busy with France and Great Britain was busy with Hitler, the Red Army stood mobilized on the Rumanian frontier. On June 26 the USSR decided that the time had come to send a firm note to Rumania asking that she withdraw her troops from Bessarabia, as she had promised to do some twenty-two years before. The Rumanian rulers looked at the Red Army and sent a call to Hitler for help. Not being ready, Hitler refused. So Rumania agreed to the Soviet proposal. Rumania troops withdrew from Bessarabia and the Red Army came in.

When the first Red Army pontoons were launched on the Dniester, peasants from Bessarabia swam out to meet them and guide them to the best landing places. "We have waited for you for twenty-two years" was the commonest greeting in the villages.

Marshal Semyon Timoshenko, commander in chief of the Red Army that entered Bessarabia, was himself a Bessarabian boy. Coming back to his home village, he found his brother Efim—who was still a poverty-stricken peasant, as their parents had been. The brothers embraced, and the villagers celebrated the return of this famous son of theirs who, while time stood still in Bessarabia, had become a marshal of the great USSR.

Many other peasants learned of peasant relatives, separated for twenty-two years by the border, who had meanwhile become engineers or government officials in the USSR. Village women of Bessarabia stared in astonishment at the women doctors who came with the Red Army, some of them with medals on their breasts.

Two-thirds of the people of Bessarabia were Moldavians, the rest being largely Ukrainians and Jews. The new territory was therefore combined with the sixty-mile-square Moldavia, which was asked to provide teachers, organizers, engineers, for an area six times its former size. The enlarged area became a sovereign republic of the USSR, its representatives being seated in the Supreme Soviet in the Kremlin on August 2, 1940. It was thus the thirteenth Soviet Republic, being at once followed by the three Baltic States.

Federal funds were sent at once to the new republic for agriculture, industry, and education. Tractors and modern farm machines came in to work the soil. Schools were set up in the villages, teaching in the Moldavian tongue. Organization went on with feverish speed. Everyone knew that the time was short in which to prepare for the great struggle, that Rumania had given up Bessarabia unwillingly, and that Rumanian troops were waiting just beyond the Pruth River until Hitler should be ready for war.

Less than a year from the day when Bessarabian peasants were seated in the Kremlin Palace as deputies from "great Moldavia," Hitler's armies and those of Rumania attacked the Soviet frontier. Moldavia was one of the first areas conquered, and one of the last to be freed.

Fifty thousand Jews were shot in Moldavia in the first months of Nazi occupation. This area was part of the old "Pale of Settlement" to which the Russian tsars exiled the Jews. Its cities had a large Jewish population. "There is not a Jew left in Bessarabia," boasted a Rumanian newspaper a few months after the Nazi armies came.

Many Moldavians retreated with the Red Army. Others fought as guerrillas. This territory is not as well adapted to guerrilla fighting as the woods and swamps of the northern countries; it is too open and flat. Moldavia was too far behind the German lines to receive much help by air from the main Red Army. Nonetheless Moldavia had its hero guerrillas.

Twenty-year-old Nikolai Frolov organized a detachment that derailed and blew up fourteen German troop trains within three months, killing several thousand enemy troops. Vasili Timoshuk, a somewhat older farmer, formed a detachment that wrecked eleven troop trains, burned an oil train, and blew up two bridges. These two guerrillas were given the decoration of "Hero of the Soviet Union."

During nearly three years of occupation, and especially during their final retreat, the Germans and Rumanians looted thoroughly this territory which they knew they would never again possess. But they could not take the fertile soil from Moldavia. And this fertile soil is Moldavia's greatest wealth.

It was springtime when the Red Army returned. It was spring of the year 1944, when the Red Army made the great advance to its frontiers and beyond them to meet its allies of the west. Even in devastated Moldavia, springtime was beautiful with promise that this fertile country, now at peace, could repair the many ravages of war.

WHITE RUSSIANS, THE PEOPLE BETWEEN
THE MARSHES

THE FOLK SONGS of the White Russians are mournful. This is
due in part to their dreary landscape and impoverished past, and
in part to long centuries of alien rule. Only some of the modern
songs are jolly and full of jokes.

The White Russians are Slavs, tall, sturdy, and blond. Some
hold that they are the purest Slav type. But they never had a
sovereign state of their own until after the Russian Revolution
of 1917. For seven hundred years they were under Lithuanian
and Polish overlords. Yet they clung to their unity as a people,
through their language, their folk songs, and their religion.

The Republic of White Russia is somewhat larger than Minnesota with more than three times as many people. Its area is nearly 90,000 square miles; its population, over 10,000,000. It lies east of Poland, Lithuania, and Latvia, separating these countries from Russia. The straight-line railway from Berlin to Moscow passes through Minsk, the White Russian capital, which is a little more than halfway.

In White Russia the wet winds from the Atlantic meet the cold dry air of the Russian plain, causing heavy rains in spring and autumn and damp, penetrating cold in winter. These rains have determined the country's condition and history. For the land is a watershed between streams that flow northwest to the Baltic and others that flow south to the Black Sea. Since the watershed is low, the heavy rains not only fill the rivers but flood widely into marshes that cover more than one-fifth of the entire territory. The most famous are the great Pripet marshes in the southern part of the republic. They have blocked the movements of men and of nations for centuries.

The White Russians live between the marshes, in forest clearings of indifferent soil. Most of them live on the higher lands in the center between the marshes of the north and those of the south. But since the nobles have taken the better ground for centuries, White Russian peasants pushed even into the Pripet marshes to live on sandy hillocks wrapped in mists and vapors and surrounded by the bog.

In that monotonous marshland—it is called Polessia—each tiny hamlet is shut off from its neighbors for most of the year. During spring floods they go from island to island in canoes driven by sail or paddle or pulled across shallows by long-horned oxen. In summer they cannot travel at all. Only when winter freezes the marshes is there firm travel over the snow. Then peasants venture out to trade their scanty harvest for salt, matches, and a bit of cotton goods. Matches are so precious that they are split into four parts before being struck. Salt is so precious that the salt water in which potatoes have been boiled is kept for many boilings for weeks.

Not all of White Russia is as harsh as Polessia. There are many pleasant farmlands along the wider rivers. The western Dvina tumbles northward in rapids toward the great Riga Bay. The silver Dnieper flows majestically southward; it has more than a thousand miles to go to the Black Sea. The blue Berezina runs merrily the whole length of the republic; it is the historic river of White Russia whose depths have drowned many thousands of invaders. The lands along these rivers grow flax and hemp and potatoes and rye. But even these lands are not easy to farm. They are often flooded in spring. They are separated by marshes.

The White Russian peasants have lived between the marshes for centuries, down to the present day.

The Slav tribes that settled this watershed were some of those turned back by the Emperor Trajan about A.D. 100. Their choice of a home was a good enough one for those days. They were right at the portage of the great Slav trade route toward the Baltic and the Black Sea. But the choice was unlucky for their descendants—not only because the watershed was narrow, so that when the people multiplied they had to push into the swamps, but also because the narrow watershed between the marshes—where the railway to Moscow now runs—was the natural highway for Asiatic tribes migrating into Europe and for Poles and Germans pushing east.

From the earliest days of the Slavs the people between the marshes were separate principalities who joined the other Slavs for purposes of war. They took part in the famous campaign of Kiev-Russ against Constantinople and shared in the loot. The

Mongol invasion that burned Kiev in 1240 was halted by the marshes. The people between the marshes remained free. Some authorities hold that the name "Byelo-Russian"—White Russian—comes from that period and was used to describe their independence from Mongol rule (the word "white" has a secondary meaning, "free"). Others hold that it came from their long whitish clothing, homespun from their flax. Still others think that it was given because they were more blond than the Russians, who had an admixture of Finnish blood, or than the Ukrainians, who had intermarried with Mongols and Turks.

All this was sharply changed by the royal marriage that united Lithuania and Poland in 1569. One of the terms of the marriage was that the Lithuanian king and all his subjects should embrace Roman Catholicism, the faith of the Poles. The White Russian peasants stuck to their own religion, in spite of bishop, pope, or king. They had received the Orthodox variety of Christianity straight from "Holy Kiev," which had it from the Eastern Empire and the old Greek Church. The men of the marshes were a stubborn folk. They have fought that "Polish religion" from 1569 down to the present day.

On the day when Lenin took power in Petersburg, November 7, 1917, a group of workingmen in Minsk proclaimed a Soviet government for White Russia. Peasants began to divide the nobles' estates. But this early government had a short life because the Germans advanced into this territory. They were, however, driven out and on January 1, 1919, White Russia became a separate Soviet Republic.

Twenty million acres of land in Soviet White Russia that had belonged to the tsar, the nobles, and the monasteries were distributed at once to the peasants and farm hands who were tilling it. When added to the 15,000,000 acres the peasants already possessed this gave them more than twice as much as before. The new land was much better and more conveniently located. During the next ten years the peasants organized cooperative farms with the help of government credits and machines. The cultivated area rapidly increased from 6,250,-000 acres to 10,000,000 by 1937. Nearly 9000 tractors and thousands of harvester combines, potato seeders, and cultivators were used in the cooperative fields. The harvest yield doubled, giving the people four times as much food as before.

The change in the rural districts can be shown from two villages.

Mokhoed is a village in the southern marshes. Its name means "moss-eater." Its people actually ate moss, as did those of many of the poorer villages. The near-by meadows and cultivated land belonged to the lord. The peasants owned some swampy woodland eight to ten miles away. Here they dried the moss, collected acorns, and mixed the two with chaff from the landlord's rye. Thus they made bread. The village suffered from all kinds of epidemics and seemed constantly on the point of dying out. Then a cooperative farm was formed.

By 1938 Mokhoed was thriving. The cooperative farmers produced good food on the former landlord's estate, but the chief income came from the two new sawmills established during the Five Year Plans. There was a hospital in the village, and a clubhouse with motion pictures; there were five schools in its scattered hamlets. There were radios in most of the homes. The birth rate shows the improvement: in 1934 seventeen babies were born, in 1937 about a hundred.

Dashkova lies in the better lands; it was a typical White Russian farm region. The peasants farmed tiny strips surrounded by a large area of land belonging to the lord. The priest wrote most of the letters for the villagers, few of whom could read and write. There was a parish school for forty pupils; it had three grades, and taught a little reading and writing and the Catechism to the children of the better-off peasants. In the stagnant life most of them soon forgot the little they learned. For centuries not a single villager ever became anything but a farm laborer or a shepherd.

Today everyone in Dashkova can read and write. There are evening schools and a township high school with more than four hundred pupils. Young folks go away to college on scholarships. The village has already produced from its children eight teachers, seven doctors, five lieutenants of the Red Army, two engineers, a pilot, an agronomist, a diplomat, and dozens of tractor drivers and mechanics.

It is pleasant when twilight falls on the wide meadows of the cooperative farm to stand on the nearest hillock or old burial mound and watch the lights come on in the farm buildings. The windows of homes, of evening schools, of the club building and the stables, are bright with electric light. You hear the sound of old songs and new songs. Some of the new songs have a pleasant humor.

White Russia's good fortune comes today directly from its swamps. More than 2,000,000 acres of them have been drained under Soviet rule. Some of this area makes good farmland. The rest of it makes good peat supply. This is important wealth. Peat is good fuel. Peat is also good fertilizer, especially for sandy soil. Many important industrial chemicals are obtained from peat.

The two curses of the White Russian farmlands are the peat swamps and the sandy hillocks. These two worst soils were mixed together and very good soil was secured. The fine long flax of White Russia grows well on such soil. White Russian flax is exported and is famous throughout the world.

Electric power stations were built near the peat swamps, using the peat for fuel. Some cooperative farms even had their

Town and country in White Russia—a peat machine at work in a rural area and a view of the new government buildings in Minsk

own electric power plant in their own swamp. Large power stations supplied the 2000 new industrial establishments that were built in White Russia from 1928 to 1937, the years of the two Five Year Plans. By 1939 White Russia was producing from its swamps nearly half a million kilowatt-hours of energy, more than a hundred times as much electricity as the area had in 1913. The swamps that were once the source of misery and poverty had become the source of light and power.

In the old days there was little industry in White Russia. White Russian products today go to all parts of the USSR. Its paper mills make it possible for children far away in Central Asia to have plenty of textbooks. Its cement built the massive walls of the great Moscow-Volga Canal. Its tiles and flagstones ornament the beautiful Moscow subway. Its prefabricated houses supply new homes in the Arctic, in Kazakhstan and the Far East.

The capital of the White Russian Republic is a very ancient town, an old trading post between the tribes of Azerbaidjan and the western people of Europe. The word "mensk" means "to trade." Under the tsars Minsk became a ghetto town in which two-fifths of the people were Jews. There was no water or sewer system; there were no streetcars or electric lights—for a city of nearly a hundred thousand people. There were public wells in some of the streets, and stinking outhouses in the back yards. A small commercial college gave Jews their only chance for higher education. Rich Jews could send their sons on condition of supporting two poor Russians for every Jewish boy.

In 1938 there were 20,000 students in a score of higher institutions of learning, including a law school, a conservatory of music, an agricultural college. An imposing ten-story structure of modernistic architecture housed government offices. Not far away stood the gray stone opera house, the yellow stone agricultural academy, the White Russian Academy of Science, the big central labor temple, the "cooperative farm center," and the national library whose 2,000,000 volumes were supplied by free delivery to all the hamlets of White Russia. "Mosquito Hole," a former swamp and dump heap at the edge of town, had been covered by scores of fine apartment houses. A special "Hospital Town" just outside Minsk centralized the hospital care for all the rural districts of White Russia.

Schools, universities, and government posts were open on equal terms to all citizens. Jews were admitted like any other students. To promote or advocate race discrimination was a punishable crime.

For Hitler's troops White Russia lay on the straight road to Moscow. It suffered his first and strongest blow. The German armies overran the entire republic and held it for more than three years. Few people from this area had time to escape to the east.

White Russian farmers became guerrilla fighters. Their woods and swamps are adapted to such fighting. After two years of war White Russians in the Red Army addressed their fellow countrymen by radio across the German lines. They stated that there were 108 White Russian generals in the Red Army, as well as hundreds of thousands of Red Army men. They announced that the fighting farmer guerrillas of White Russia, operating entirely behind German lines, had derailed several hundred German troop trains; blown up more than 1000 bridges; killed to date 180,000 Germans, including 13 generals.

The first fighting farmers to win the title "Hero of the Soviet Union" were two men of the White Russian swamps.

KARELIA, LAND OF THE NORTH STAR

AN OLD SONG sung by the minstrels of Karelia says the god of the polar star governs an insignificant spot in the vault of the sky, but in this spot he knows no master. The good sturdy people of Karelia are like the polar star of whom they sing.

Sprung from an ancient race—for they are one of the Finnish tribes that drifted westward from the valley of the Volga and then north—the Karelians have clung to their indifferent soil for more than fifteen hundred years and have remained master of it.

The Soviet Karelo-Finn Republic is only a small part of the territory over which the early Karelians hunted, fished, and waged endless wars against plunderers and invaders. It is some

64,000 square miles in area, about the size of Maine, New Hampshire, and Vermont together. It is a long, narrow strip of country that begins a little to the east of Leningrad and runs north for almost 1000 miles between Finland and the White Sea. It is thus one of the most northerly lands in the world and is sparsely settled, having less than 900,000 people all told. Its climate is not only cold but very damp.

Karelia is a land of lakes and forests. Karelians tell you that they have a lake for the back yard of every family; there are actually some 35,000 lakes and ponds, one for every thirteen persons. These include the two largest lakes in Europe: Lake Ladoga, which forms part of Karelia's border with Finland, and Lake Onega—on which lies the capital, Petrozavodsk. Some 15 per cent of Karelia's entire area consists of rivers and lakes.

All around the lakes lie the forests; they cover two-thirds of the country and are its greatest wealth. They are mostly tall dark pine trees brightened by the delicate white trunks of birches. They abound in wild life, both game and birds. Karelia is known as the "land of unfrightened birds." In the still white summer night the call of the cuckoo is heard from the deep shadowy forest, while with dawn the wild swans, geese, and ducks rise from the forest lakes. In the southern part of the country some of the forest has been cleared away; here lies the principal farming region. In the northern part the forest grows sparse as it approaches the Arctic.

The ice of the Glacial Age tore Karelia into many rocky ridges, which cross and recross irregularly. These, together with the lakes and marshes, make travel very difficult; but they supply rich mineral wealth, especially all kinds of marble, granite, limestone, feldspar, and quartz. The mica mines have been known for centuries; the oldest palace in the Kremlin of

Moscow still has windows that were made of mica in the days before Russia had glass. Karelia also produces its own fuel; it has a practically endless supply of peat.

The Karelians came to this area long before written records were made. They drove out the nomadic Lapps, who today live in the northern and less desirable regions. Karelians built log houses. Their houses differ from those of the Russians; they are built for colder and damper climate. They have two stories; the horses and cattle live downstairs and the people upstairs. This is warmer for both man and beast in the seven long months of winter; the man can feed his cattle without going outdoors. It is also safer, for the people and cattle are both protected from wild beasts of the forest. But the houses are gloomy and weather-beaten; paint was never known in this land.

Ten or twelve such houses in a clearing form a Karelian village. One house is set aside from the others and is only one story high. This is the community bathhouse. A Karelian takes his bath in company. He produces a steam bath by placing red-hot stones on the ground and pouring over them the icy lake water. He beats his friend from head to foot with bunches of birch and willow twigs while the steaming friend returns the courtesy. They joke and exchange village gossip. All emerge from the bath beet-red, clean as a whistle, and in a pleasantly relaxed frame of mind.

The only village structure that has any claim to beauty is the Karelian church. Its odd mixture of conflicting kinds of architecture has excited the interest of architects in all lands. The onion-shaped dome of the Russian church, which came originally from the warm climate of Constantinople, is cunningly contrived of wooden shingles by the Karelians and is perched on the precipitous roofs and among the sharp steeples that characterize the Gothic architecture of northern Europe. These strange churches have a peculiar fitness in the Karelian land-scape, with its many rounded hills and tall pointed pines. They also fit Karelia's long history, in which the conflicts of the Slavs with the Scandinavians intertwine.

Even in their early days of primitive poverty the Karelians preserved their folklore and mythology in songs which today form one of the great epics of the European peoples. The *Kale-vala* was not written down until the nineteenth century. It contains early myths common to all the Finnish tribes, but most of its runes, or verses, were collected from peasant minstrels of Karelia. Longfellow borrowed its meter for *Hiawatha*, finding in it a rhythm of universal appeal:

> Mastered by an inward urging
> I am ready for the chanting
> Of our nation's ancient folk song
> Handed down from bygone ages,
> Seldom do we come for singing,
> Seldom to the one, the other,
> O'er this cold and cruel country,
> O'er the poor soil of the northland.

The *Kalevala* tells of the bitter struggle of the people for grain, salt, and gold and is embroidered with very beautiful and imaginative description. Otso, the bear, for instance, was nursed by a goddess of the woodlands in a cradle "swung by bands of gold between the branches of the budding firs." The language of the Karelians is full of such imaginative imagery.

When Kiev-Russ adopted Christianity the missionaries of the Greek Orthodox Church spread northward into Karelia also. They set up monasteries which not only preached Christianity but levied taxes and carried on farming with imported Russian and also native serfs. The most powerful monastery of the north was at Solovietsky, an island in the White Sea. It had its own army and a fortress with very thick walls; its port on the Karelian mainland at Kem bristled with three more forts. A second strong monastery was at Petsamo on the Arctic coast, founded by missionaries from Novgorod.

For centuries the Karelians regarded these monasteries as an oppressive foreign importation; they kept on worshiping their own gods—the sun, the moon, and other nature deities in the deep woods. During the period of peasant wars—the sixteenth to seventeenth century—a Karelian guerrilla leader, Juho Vesainen, surprised the monks at Petsamo and completely destroyed their monastery. He successfully raided most of the other strongholds of the Russian Church, but Solovietsky held fast; the doughty Juho broke his stout heart against its impregnable walls.

The Russian tsars spent centuries trying to Russianize the Karelians. Church services were held in Church Slavonic; to sell a Bible written in Finnish was punishable by exile. Schools were taught only in Russian; children were punished for speaking Karelian even in the schoolgrounds. The stubborn Karelians boycotted these schools; less than 10 per cent of them learned to read and write. These conditions prevailed in Karelia up to the Russian Revolution.

When the Russian Revolution of 1917 granted self-determination to the minor nationalities, the Finnish government in Helsinki seceded. The Karelians remained under Soviet rule and in July, 1920, the elected delegates from Karelian villages met in Petrozavodsk and expressed the desire to become an autonomous republic, part of the Russian Soviet Federated Socialist Republic. They remained an autonomous republic under the REFSR until 1940; then the territory taken from Finland in the Russo-Finnish War was added to Karelia, which became the Karelo-Finn Republic, a sovereign state with the right to secede.

Karelia is strategically very important to the USSR as the land through which the railroad runs from Leningrad to the Arctic port at Murmansk; it has gained additional importance by the building of the Baltic-White Sea Canal, which connects Leningrad directly with the Arctic by water without leaving the territory of the USSR.

The territory that became Soviet Karelia was one of the most backward parts of the USSR. In 1922 only one farming family in seven had even a metal blade for its plow. With such primitive implements the poor northern soil gave scanty harvests. The people of Karelia were always hungry. They ate "bark bread" made by extending their meager barley and rye with the inner pulp of pine bark.

Barges were still being made in Petrozavodsk by the ancient method of Peter the Great. The timbers were ax-hewn; no saw was used. Instead of metal pipes they made wooden pipes by boring down the length of nine-foot timbers; the special bore took three men to operate it. They were proud of this craft; they fought the introduction of iron pipes and machines.

Incredibly rapid changes followed that difficult beginning. By 1939 the population had doubled. This was due to the better food. A farm experiment station replaced the old monastery at Solovietsky; other stations were located in various parts of Karelia, while the famous Arctic farm which lies two hundred miles north of the Arctic Circle is near enough to Karelia so that its new varieties of grain and potatoes and vegetables are available to Karelian farms. With better seed, modern machinery, and thousands of acres reclaimed by drainage, Karelia now produces its own bread. The primitive implements have gone to museums.

By 1939 the air over Petrozavodsk—Peter's Factory—was noisy with airplanes; here lay the crossroads of several Arctic routes. Munitions for the Red Army came by conveyor system from a plant that once made guns for Peter the Great. The swiftest skis for the Red Army were also made here from Karelian birch. Farther north in the deep forests the icy brown torrents of rivers rushed into the intake of giant turbines that were usually stamped "made in America." The long polar night was lighted by electricity so that the hum of sawmills and the drilling in mines and quarries was never forced to rest.

By 1939 education had been for several years compulsory through the grammar grades. Besides 500 grade schools there were 60 high schools, 11 technical schools, 3 institutions of higher learning. Almost every house in the woods had a radio; every village had a meeting house where motion pictures were shown and traveling players put on classic and modern plays.

A unique contribution was made by some 5000 Finnish-Americans who went to Karelia from the United States and Canada from 1920 to 1933. Soviet Karelia invited them to come and teach the ways of modern industry. They were skilled loggers, woodworkers, building and metal workers. They had many troubles with the industrial methods of Peter the Great and with stubborn Karelians who didn't want to be told their business by outsiders, even by Americanized Finns. Some of the Americans went back to America disappointed; others remained. All of them hastened Karelia toward modern technique. One can still hear the "American language" in the most distant corners of Karelia. No spot in the woods was too remote for these lumberjacks from the American northwest.

At a place called Shunga on Lake Onega is a mine that is operated entirely by American Finns. It is a schungite mine, said to be the only one in the world. Schungite is a silvery ore used as

Women at an old-fashioned sewing bee, a modern lumberjack, and a
meteorologist, all contribute to daily living in Karelia

a substitute for graphite and also to produce vanadium for the manufacture of steel. Before the Americans took charge it required seventy-two hours to load a barge with schungite by hand. The Americans built a wharf with an ore chute; after this a barge could be loaded in one hour.

The most famous new construction in Karelia was not built by Karelians. It is the Baltic-White Sea Canal built by the federal government of the USSR. It is almost as important strategically to the USSR as the Panama Canal is to the United States.

Formerly a steamer going from Leningrad to the Arctic had to swing all the way around the Scandinavian peninsula. By the new 141 mile canal and the rivers connecting with it, steamers from Leningrad to Archangel pass directly across Soviet territory—making the trip in three or four days instead of the former seventeen days. This great canal was built in the record time of twenty-one months and was finished in 1933. It was a great link in the northern sea route around Asia, whose development occupied the next ten years.

The canal's greatest publicity in the Soviet Union came from another reason. It was built entirely by convict labor. It was announced as a great experiment in "reforging human beings" not only by ordinary work but by the inspiration of a great patriotic task. Tens of thousands of convicts from all parts of the USSR were sent to the Karelian woods and scattered over its vast expanse. All the wardens, all the foremen, even all the engineers, had to be drawn from the ranks of convicts, which included not only thieves and murderers but engineers convicted of sabotage against publicly owned industries.

The experiment succeeded. The canal was built so brilliantly that the government decided to reward the convict builders. Twelve thousand men had their sentences canceled; most of the others, to the number of sixty thousand, had their sentences greatly reduced. Hundreds won high decorations; men who had thought themselves disgraced for life went home in triumph. Gangs of the "canal soldiers" were wanted everywhere on construction work. Forty leading Soviet authors, under the chairmanship of Maxim Gorky, visited the canal and wrote up its success in the "reforging of men." Kirghiz bandits from Central Asia, thieves and bootleggers from the cities, went home to brag to their old associates: "With pickaxes, my dears, we dug it so that all America and Europe gasped and took off its hat!"

The Baltic-White Sea Canal opened the forests of Karelia to such easy access that the timber output doubled almost at once, rising in 1939 to eight times the highest record of the pre-Soviet years. The canal also opened the great but desolate Kola peninsula north of Karelia; connected its raw materials with Karelian man power, enabling the peasants of the northern woods to find year-round jobs in developing new riches of the north.

The Kola peninsula—with the Arctic port of Murmansk—is part of the RSFSR and, though not of the Karelo-Finn Republic, is closely bound to it. The *Kalevala* describes it as the "land of eternal gloom," the "land of shadows," the "land of sleep." Here the straggly forests die out into the melancholy underbrush and treacherous mosses of the Arctic. The workers along the railway here are garbed fantastically with black masks on their faces and long white mantles shrouding their bodies. They are not dressed for a masque ball; they are protected against mosquitoes, which do not fight singly but in cruel massed formation in this land.

Here in this desolation, under perpetual daylight in summer and the long unbroken winter night, lie great deposits of apatite, which is useful for fertilizer and many industrial needs.

The deposits have been known since the sixteenth century but were never developed until today. They are estimated at two billion tons, the largest apatite deposits in the world. A new town named Kirovsk has grown up on the Kola peninsula; its output of apatite reached three million tons in 1936. Transportation into Karelia is cheap because of the new canal, so chemical industries based on apatite were developed there. Karelia today stands high in the chemical industry of the USSR. Power plants on Karelian rivers, built to serve the new industries, have increased Karelia's electric power from 700 kilowatts in pre-Soviet days to 40,000 in 1940.

The most northerly in the chain of Arctic farm experimental stations lies two hundred miles north of the Arctic circle near Kirovsk. To produce northern grain the station tested ten thousand varieties of wheat and barley and selected ten of each. By crossing Algerian, Tunisian, Alaskan, and Norwegian grains it developed a grain that will mature quickly in the sixty-five to eighty frostless days of the polar lands. It also uses the method of "vernalization" developed by the Ukrainian scientist Lysenko; this consists in bringing the seed almost to the point of sprouting before it is planted. The station also developed a potato which survives at six degrees below freezing; in order to produce it an expedition was sent to South America for the sturdy wild potatoes of the mountains, which were then crossed with the common garden variety.

All these new varieties spread rapidly into northern farmlands not only in Karelia but even on the Kola peninsula, where man has never farmed before. More than 7000 acres were cultivated on Kola in 1940. This experiment is no attempt to compete with the great farms of the southern parts of the USSR. It is intended as a lifesaver for the 2,000,000 people who live and work today in the Soviet Arctic and who need fresh vege-

This reindeer-breeding farm, 108 miles north of the Arctic Circle, is near the port of Murmansk where these trawlers lie at anchor

tables in their battle against scurvy, the dreaded disease of the north.

The Arctic port of Murmansk on the Kola peninsula became a key city in the war plans of the United Nations during the second World War. Lend-lease shipments were sent into Murmansk, which because of the Gulf Stream remains ice-free all the year. This north Atlantic route proved very dangerous because Petsamo—the old port founded in the Middle Ages by monks from Novgorod and given by Soviet Russia to Finland in 1918—became a German submarine and airplane base. Many American and other ships of the United Nations were sunk in the Arctic before they could reach Murmansk. The largest ship repairyard in the USSR was built at Murmansk to repair damaged ships.

One group of American seaman escaped from a torpedoed ship and came by raft to Novaya Zemlia, the barren Arctic island that stretches toward the pole. Their lives were saved by a camp of Russian children who were spending their summer vacation collecting ducks and duck eggs for the needs of the front. The oldest were fifteen years and the youngest were only eight; they managed their own camp without adults, since all grown-up people had other tasks for the war. These children shared their food with the Americans and also showed the Americans how to snare ducks for meat, how to tell good eggs from bad ones, where to find safe drinking water, and how to live fairly well in the desolate Arctic country.

Thus the help given by Americans in developing Karelia and the northern USSR was repaid to other Americans in the bitter days of war.

THE BALTIC STATES, WINDOWS ON EUROPE

IN THE SECOND YEAR of the Hitler invasion a nation-in-exile met in Moscow to honor its national holiday. The little Baltic Republic of Estonia had been occupied for twenty months by German troops. Six hundred miles from their homeland its representatives celebrated St. George Night, commemorating the earliest Estonian revolt against German invaders in 1343.

"The flame of St. George Night has blazed in the breast of every Estonian for six hundred years," declared Johannes Vares, the poet president of the republic. "Again and again these same brutal invaders strove to extinguish our people utterly from the earth. But the Estonian people will rise again. We fight not alone but in comradeship of arms with all the peoples of the USSR."

Applauding him were commanders and men of Estonian units of the Red Army; managers of Estonian factories that had temporarily moved a thousand miles to the Urals; scientists, actors, and artists who had come to Moscow "for the duration"; teachers who taught refugee Estonian children in their own language in special Moscow schools. Men and women guerrillas came to this meeting across the German lines from the Baltic forests. They were continuing a six-century-old tradition, striking at Germans from the woods.

The three Baltic Republics—Estonia, Latvia, and Lithuania—lie on the eastern shore of the Baltic Sea. Taken together they are in size and population equal to New England without the metropolitan area of Boston. Their 6,000,000 people live on 66,714 square miles of northern woods and meadows. Latvia, the central republic, is largest in area—25,402 square miles—and possesses the important port of Riga. Lithuania, the southernmost, is largest in population; its 2,879,070 people include its much-disputed capital, Vilna. Estonia, the northern republic, is smallest in area and population but guards the Gulf of Finland, which is the sea approach to Leningrad.

The common location of these three countries has given them a common history. They are bounded by Prussia and Poland on the south, by Russia on the east. Bloody wars have been waged for their possession since the twelfth century. In only a few of these wars have the native peoples played a deciding part.

The first German invasions of this area were followed by the crusade of the Teutonic Knights approved by Pope Innocent III in 1204. After converting two of the heathen tribes, the knights took over their land in the name of the Pope. Twenty years later they began a series of conquests which gradually changed their original semireligious character to a purely military and administrative one. German Nazis today claim these early crusaders as the "foremost heroes of German history who endeavored to give us living space in the east."

To the Baltic peoples these "Black Knights," so called from the color of their armor, were a terror that endured seven hundred years in some areas. Every Baltic child learns of them as pitiless conquerors who burned villages; killed men, women, and children; made slaves of freedom-loving folk. The "Black Knights" slaughtered almost to a man the tribe known as Borussians and took their land for a German stronghold. It is East Prussia today.

Attempts of these early conquerors to drive farther into Russia were defeated in 1242 by Alexander Nevsky, prince of Novgorod, in the famous "battle on the ice." Attempts to drive southeast into the Ukrainian lands were defeated by the Lithuanians in a conflict that lasted two hundred years. One of the most glorious pages of Lithuanian history is the battle of Grünwald in 1410, when Lithuanian grand dukes led an alliance of Russians, Ukrainians, White Russians, Poles, and Czechs and routed the "Black Knights." This victory made Lithuania the leader of eastern Europe for a century and a half. She was then absorbed by an expanding Poland and in the eighteenth century by the Russian Empire. German armies have often overrun Lithuanian territory but have never been abiding rulers in her land.

In Latvia and Estonia the Germans remained as rulers. The Order of Teutonic Knights was dissolved in 1561, but its members did not go home. They stayed on as "Baltic barons," supporting whatever great state would recognize their feudal privileges. In the seventeenth century Sweden ruled the area, encouraged education, and forbade trading in serfs. The Baltic barons, disliking these progressive tendencies, helped Peter the Great defeat Sweden. Estonia and part of Latvia were added to the Russian Empire in 1721. A grateful tsardom restored all the feudal privileges that Sweden had denied the barons, including the right to take any village bride on her wedding night. Two hundred German families were given the sole right to possess land in the Baltic States.

In the tsar's court the Baltic barons became very powerful. They organized the tsar's "Black Hundreds," which later formed the model for Hitler's "Gestapo." They did not, however, enjoy an undisturbed rule in the Baltic States. The red thread of peasant rebellion runs through the entire seven hundred years of Latvian and Estonian history, from the first famous uprising of St. George Night, in 1343, down through the nineteenth and twentieth centuries.

"I'll forgive anyone but I won't forgive a German" runs a Lettish song.

The revolutionary uprisings that swept through Russia in 1905 were especially violent in the Baltic States. The German barons personally supervised the ruthless suppression, burning villages, shooting scores of hostages, and hanging teachers in the presence of their students. Baltic peasants fled to the woods and organized fighting bands known as "forest brothers."

From that dark night of terror came the dawn of a new hope for the Baltic peoples' freedom through the wider fight of the Russian people. The aim of the national movements in Latvia, Lithuania, Estonia, and even in Finland, became national autonomy within a free and democratic Russia. Many Latvian fighters went to the scaffold crying: "A free Latvia in a free Russia!"

All three Baltic States were occupied by German armies in the first World War. This time the Germans planned to stay and colonize the land. They calculated how many millions of Germans could here find "living space." "The Lettish peasants will disappear. A small nation like the Letts will be in no position to offer resistance," reported one German administrator. Thousands of Baltic people fled into Russia. The tsar, knowing their deep hatred for Germans, formed special Baltic regiments. These won glory in the World War and later became some of the best shock troops of the Russian Revolution.

Soviet Republics were set up in the Baltic States on November 7, 1917, the day when revolution occurred in Leningrad. They were short-lived. Germany took the Baltic lands from a defeated Russia through the treaty of Brest-Litovsk. When Germany collapsed at the end of 1918, Soviet Republics again appeared in the Baltic. The defeated Germans profited from the Allies' fear of the "Bolshevik menace." They were asked by the allied victors to put down the Baltic revolution. German troops with allied assistance helped set up "independent governments" in Finland, Latvia, Estonia, and Lithuania.

For several years these new Baltic governments were not officially recognized by the allied powers that brought them into being. Clemenceau, the French representative, frankly called them a "policy of barbed-wire entanglements from the Arctic Ocean to the Black Sea." They were used as a military base against Soviet Russia; it was expected that they would be returned to Russia after the Bolsheviks were overthrown. Soviet Russia was the first to recognize them, signing treaties with them in 1920 in order to secure peace. The United States finally recognized them in 1922, officially indicating the belief that they would someday become part of a federated Russia since their economic life was bound with the Russian hinterland.

The new independent states began with high hopes. Through democracy they expected the benefits of the Russian Revolution without its excesses. The young governments took land from the German barons to distribute to peasants. The farmers copied the cooperatives of Sweden and Denmark. Native intellectuals rose to government posts, achieving some remarkable progress.

Deep at the heart of all this democratic achievement gnawed the cancer of an upper class that was still largely German. Its influence worked at first indirectly. Its aim was to separate the Baltic peoples from Russia. Since industry and commerce could not survive in these states without close relations with Russia, the German-influenced upper class preferred to see the ports and industries shut down. "Down with heavy industry" actually became a slogan of politicians who encouraged the little countries to live by selling farm products to foreign lands.

Shipyards and car-building works closed for lack of Russian orders. Once-busy ports became desolate for want of Russian freight. Great railway junctions became ghost towns. Chronic unemployment afflicted the Baltic cities. Everywhere else in the world modern industry was increasing, but in Latvia the number of industrial workers fell from 108,000 in 1913 to 62,000 in the boom year of 1929. Butter, bacon, and timber became the Baltic products. This was what Germany desired. From 60 to 70 per cent of Baltic wholesale trade came into German hands.

The collapse of the world market in 1930 deeply shook the unstable Baltic economy. Political disturbances followed; fascist regimes were set up on the Nazi model. Democracy had no deep-rooted traditions in the Baltic and had been undermined from the beginning. It was crushed in Lithuania in 1926 by a conspiracy of army officers; in Estonia in 1934 by the chief of state with the help of the army; in Latvia in the same year by army men and politicians under the direct instruction of German Nazis, from whom they adopted even the Hitler salute. All three Baltic governments dissolved parliaments and threw opponents into concentration camps. How could these weak new democracies withstand a Nazi penetration that was strong enough to undermine the great republican tradition of France?

All the Baltic States, including Finland, next became a military base for Hitler's plans against Russia. Forts set up on the Russian border were inspected by General Halder, chief of the German General Staff. German specialists superintended the building of an airdrome near Riga—and similar ones in Finland —ten times as large as the native air force could use. Army officers suspected of anti-Nazi feelings were purged. Politicians of the Baltic States were bribed by shares in German companies or hypnotized by a vision of the "invincible Germany" that even Great Britain and France in those days tried to appease.

On March 15, 1939, the armies of Hitler marched into disarmed Prague and took over Czechoslovakia, an insolent breaking of all agreements. Seven days later Hitler seized Memel, Lithuania's only port on the Baltic Sea.

The Baltic people awaited the future with horror. Peasants already heard the crack of the barons' whip. Workers expected forced labor under German overseers. Jews awaited pogroms. The once-hopeful democratic intellectuals of Baltic nationality knew that Hitler Germany would treat them as an outcast "inferior race."

"We wish to live at peace with the Baltic peoples, but if these tiny countries allow big adventurers to use their territories for big adventures we shall widen our little window on Europe with the help of the Red Army," bluntly declared Andrei Zhdanov, chairman of the Foreign Affairs Committee of the USSR. The "little window" was Leningrad. A widened window meant the Baltic States.

The Baltic governments were the rock on which the hopes of Anglo-Soviet joint action against Hitler were dashed to pieces in the fateful summer of 1939. British and French representatives were in Moscow discussing an alliance against Hitler aggressions. The USSR demanded that the agreement should protect not only Holland and Belgium, as strategic outposts of Great Britain, but also the Baltic States, as strategic outposts of the USSR. The Estonian and Latvian governments chose this moment to sign an agreement with Nazi Germany on June 7, 1939. Prime Minister Chamberlain of Great Britain thereupon stated: "One cannot guarantee a state against its will." Russia knew from this that she must handle the threat to her border alone; she postponed trouble by a nonaggression pact with Hitler. The little Baltic governments were not the chief cause of world catastrophe, but they did their little best to bring it on.

The USSR acted swiftly. Taking advantage of the terror that Hitler's swift victory in Poland inspired in the Baltic peoples, Moscow proposed to the Baltic governments a defensive alliance that they did not dare refuse. Small Red Army units entered the Baltic States to strengthen the naval bases and forts built by Peter the Great. Technically they were "allies." But when Riga workers turned out to cheer these "allies," the Latvian police fired into the crowd. Men who accepted employment in building fortifications under Red Army direction were liable to arrest by their own governments. Even small boys who yelled "Hurrah for the Red Army" landed in jail.

Hitler had secured the Baltic rulers. The USSR set out to win the Baltic people in the little time that remained. From Poland's broken bits Moscow restored Vilna to the Lithuanians, who had never forgiven its illegal seizure by a Polish general twenty years before. By diplomatic channels Moscow forced Baltic Germans to return to Germany—to the number of 160,-000. This was popular with the native Baltic peoples. It also removed an enormous Nazi fifth column which was high-pressuring the Baltic governments.

Meanwhile the Red Army behaved with great correctness. It treated the little Baltic armies as equal allies, exchanging

Estonian schoolgirls laugh and giggle like schoolgirls everywhere

Latvians study a tractor schedule   Lithuanians read a "Pravda" article

military plans and dances and concerts. Peasants found that the Red Army respected peasants' property even better than their own armies did, paying at once and without question if a tank as much as smashed a farmer's fence. Workers learned that the Red Army surgeons would give unpaid help to sick civilians. Not a single scandal over drink or women developed from any Red Army post. After several months of such experience the common people began to cheer "our great ally" whenever occasion occurred.

Events moved fast in the summer of 1940. Hitler turned east from his conquest of France. He concentrated 80,000 storm troopers, disguised as "tourists," and 200 airplanes on the border of Lithuania, the nearest of the Baltic States. The USSR at once demanded that her Baltic allies admit much larger Red Army forces to strengthen their common frontier. These forces swept through the Baltic States on a few hours' notice. Crowds of citizens lined the streets. Many applauded. Several government chiefs and heads of secret police took refuge on German soil.

No disorders occurred. There were no executions. The absconding officials were replaced in the constitutional manner by the proper Baltic authorities. No member of the Red Army ever "intervened" in Baltic politics or even mentioned them. On this their instructions were strict. Outwardly the Baltic governments were the same as before except for a shift of some officials. Actually they had ceased to be outposts of Hitler and became outposts of the USSR.

Thousands of progressive leaders came home from concentration camps and began again to organize their followers. Long-suppressed trade unions came again to life. The little states seethed with meetings and discussions from border to border. Within four weeks special elections were held with by far the largest turnout of voters ever seen in the Baltic States. New parliaments met and at once applied for admission to the USSR as sovereign Soviet states.

"There are no borders any more from Kaunas to Vladivostok," said President Paletskis of Lithuania, coming from the parliament session to report to the cheering crowds.

I traveled two hundred miles on election day through Lithuania, visiting polling places. Lines formed before six in the morning in the cities; workers wanted to be the "first to vote on this historic day." Farm women walked barefoot for miles in the rain on muddy roads in the country, holding their shoes in their hands to put on clean "in honor of the election." In a town on the German border the polls were in the high school, where an election dance went on all day on the second floor. Here Lithuanian girls showed me proudly the big red "hammer and sickle" that the election committee had hung on the side of the building facing Germany.

"That's to show them over there," said the girls.

On the morning after the parliament decision the janitor at Number Six Laisves Allee pasted a strip reading "Stalino Prospect" over the former name, which by custom appeared on his house number. The janitor next door saw it; he went and did the same. By noon the main street of the Lithuanian capital was renamed from end to end by its janitors.

Moscow made the Lithuanian parliamentary decision a great occasion. An extraordinary session of the Supreme Soviet was held to receive the new states. The delegations went by special trains, met at all railway stations by bands and cheering crowds. The railway from Lithuania straight through Vilna to Moscow was opened for the first time since the Poles had closed it twenty years before. The first stop for the Lithuanians was at Minsk, capital of White Russia, where good-looking husky girls in national costumes buried the delegates under big bunches of flowers. All residents of the Baltic States were granted Soviet citizenship, including refugees from many lands—such as German and Polish Jews—who had lost their countries. The Baltic delegates were seated in the Congress of the Supreme Soviet.

In the following months the destinies of the Baltic States were guided by the presidents and parliaments that had been elected before the states became Soviet Republics. The Estonian president was Johannes Vares, a well-known poet; the Lithuanian president was Justas Paletskis, a leading journalist. The Latvian president, Professor Kirchenstein, was a scientist of international stature; the premier was Vilis Latsis, a writer so popular that when newspapers under former governments serialized his novels they had to increase their run by 30,000 copies in a country of only 2,000,000 people. The cabinet members were well-known public figures, many of whom had served in earlier democratic cabinets. Only a few were communists.

Moscow set out to prove to the Baltic peoples the advantages of being in the USSR. There were only a few months in which to do it; nobody knew how many months. But everyone knew that the time was near when the choice and the strength of the Baltic peoples would help decide the battle for the world.

The great market of the USSR absorbed rapidly everything that the Baltic States produced. In six months the chronic unemployment had entirely disappeared. The number of workers in Estonian industry on April 1, 1941, was 70 per cent higher than the previous year. A shale-oil industry was being developed with federal funds. In Latvia the shipyards were being reconditioned. In Lithuania 40 of the 84 textile mills had been idle or running part time; within six months all were running full blast and new mills were being built.

The farmers of the Baltic States were heavily burdened with mortgages, most of which, in the series of depressions, had become the property of the state. The new Soviet government canceled all these mortgages. In Latvia 115,583 farming families —a quarter of the population—were beneficiaries of this act. At the same time 19,000 new farm implements and machines came into Latvia from Russia on long-term credits.

The change in the standard of living was such that in Kaunas, which remained the Lithuanian capital while Vilna was being rebuilt, the butter consumption doubled and the amount of sausage eaten quadrupled during the first six months of Soviet rule. One hundred new schools and 66 technical high schools opened in Lithuania; 70 kindergartens, 250 playgrounds, and 4 children's theaters were established. School enrollment in Estonia rose by 11,000, in Latvia by 10,000. Four times as many books were printed in Riga, the Latvian capital, in those six months as in any previous six months in Latvian history.

Music lovers heard concerts such as had never been possible in the little, isolated countries, which few good artists could afford to tour. Grand-opera stars from Moscow and Leningrad, Russian violinists with world records, Georgian dancers, Uzbek musicians with quaint Asiatic instruments—all came now to Baltic towns. Baltic artists were invited to give concerts in Moscow. In a dozen ways the federal government told the Baltic peoples that they had joined a union of equal and sovereign nations, in which every nation's culture and art was prized.

All of them knew that just across the border stood the Nazi armies, who despised the Baltic folk as inferior races.

Twenty-four hundred children were spending vacations at the beach resort of Palanga in new children's colonies that were Lithuania's pride. At four in the morning of June 22, 1941, when all the children were sleeping, the German bombs began. The health resort became a flaming ruin in which most of the children were burned alive. Only 152 escaped to safety in the interior, sick with shattered nerves.

Thus war came to the states of the Baltic. Many cities were struck on that same day. Lighted by the flames of burning homes and factories, the people tried to move east. But the trains from Lithuania went east through White Russia, where Minsk, the stately capital that had welcomed them with flowers, was now herself in flames. Thousands of Minsk citizens were also fleeing, carrying their children on their backs into the swamps. Night came on and lost children hunted for their parents in the dark and the rain. Women dropped by the roadside to give birth. Such was the agony already in White Russia, through which the Baltic people sought to escape.

Into this agony drove the tanks of the German masters. The Baltic barons came back with the tanks. These were no mere Gestapo agents; they were men who knew every corner of the country and who had a personal hatred for the Baltic people as onetime serfs who had dared escape. They abolished the names Lithuania, Latvia, Estonia, calling them all "Ostland"—the Land of the East. "Natives" of "Ostland" were not allowed to ride on the same trains and streetcars as their masters. "Natives" received one-third the wage of Germans and less than half the food.

Slave hunts were on in the cities of the Baltic. The Germans threw a cordon around a section of a town and loaded all able-bodied men and women on freight cars for work in Germany, where hours were unlimited and punishments might be death by starvation for those who failed to please the master race. Baltic girls were forcibly put into soldiers' brothels in Germany and branded by red-hot irons with the letters SM—"Soldaten

Mädchen," or "Soldiers' Girl." A quarter of a million persons were thus taken from Lithuania for slave labor. Latvian slaves were sent to build fortifications on the Leningrad front, where a large proportion of them died of hunger and cold.

The Nazis determined to stamp out the cultural heritage of the Baltic peoples by wrecking their national libraries, burning manuscripts that had taken a generation to compile, smashing thousands of gramophone records of old Baltic folk songs. This time the "Black Knights" were making certain that nothing should be left to the slave peoples that might ever inspire them to rise.

But this time the Baltic peoples made an organized resistance such as they never before had been able to show. When the full impact of the Hitler blitzkrieg smote the Baltic peoples, not only the garrisons resisted. The population rose in arms.

The garrison at Libau was very near the frontier. Its soldiers were caught by surprise, but they held out for a week. Then, after the German armies had passed to the east, fierce street fighting broke out again in Libau streets. More than 10,000 workers of that city were shot by the Germans as "punishment."

The town of Daugavpils with only 40,000 people actually succeeded in holding up a main line of German advance. The lads of this town had never seen a tank and the flight of an airplane was to them a great event. Yet they stood up against the terrible dive bombers. Armed railway workers and Jewish people blew up the ferry across the Dvina and converted every house into a fortress that the Germans had to take street by street. Then they went into the woods as "forest brothers," as they had done against the Baltic barons nearly forty years before. This time they were not alone in their resistance. Even in the great retreat of the Red Army, the army's airplanes found time to drop supplies to the Baltic fighters in the woods.

This fighting retreat of Baltic armed units sheltered the movement of scores of thousands of Baltic people who went inland to the depths of the USSR. The Baltic States had no time to mobilize their armies. They ordered all able-bodied men to assemble in Kazakhstan and Siberia, 2000 miles to the rear. Here the national armies were formed under their own officers and sent into battle, as special units of the Red Army.

The Baltic governments were evacuated with their scientific institutions. Skeleton national universities were set up in Moscow and other Russian cities to continue the higher education of Baltic youth. Special trainloads of school children went with their teachers far into the interior and were given the summer camps of eastern cities, which they turned into winter homes and schools. Many important factories were evacuated completely, with machines, workers, and technical staff. Tens of thousands of Baltic Jews escaped to Central Asia and the Far Eastern Jewish territory of Birobidjan.

Unlike the nations of western Europe the little Baltic Republics were able not merely to send their governments-in-exile abroad. They sent "nations-in-exile," with governments, school children, factories, and armed units, preserving the continuity of their national organization for the day of return.

More than 3000 Latvians, Estonians, and Lithuanians were decorated for valor in the first two years of war. Captain Janis Wilhelms, a Latvian, killed 158 Germans himself and trained a group of snipers who accounted for 2500 more. Eighteen Latvian soldiers captured two German blockhouses and held them in continuous fighting for forty-eight hours without food or sleep until the main Red Army relieved them and found eighty dead Germans who had been killed by this single group.

Women of the Baltic States distinguished themselves both in battle and as guerrilla fighters behind the German lines. Erica

Gaile, the Latvian skiing champion, killed thirty-two Germans; Monica Meinshane killed fifty-eight. The eighteen-year-old Lithuanian girl guerrilla Maria Melnikaite organized and commanded a detachment and fought for two years before she was finally caught.

With five of her command Maria was surrounded by a large detachment of Germans. One of her comrades was killed. Maria herself in this last engagement accounted for seven Germans with her tommy gun and for several more with her grenades. She tried to blow herself up with her last grenade but was too weak from wounds to pull the pin. So the Gestapo got her and tortured her, breaking her fingers and slashing her breasts in hope of securing information. Silent under all torture, Maria was finally hanged in a Lithuanian market place as an example to the villagers.

Even in this she defeated them, for the villagers reported her last words: "What are you German dogs doing here? This is Soviet Lithuania!"

GEORGIA, LAND OF THE GOLDEN FLEECE

BEYOND THE BLACK SEA and south of the Caucasus Mountains is the place that the ancient Greeks thought of as the land of the Golden Fleece. It has had many melodious names in history; on Soviet maps you will find it shown as "Gruzia"; British geographers call it "Georgia."

It is a lovely land with every kind of scenery and climate that you can imagine, from eternal snow on the mountains of the Caucasus to eternal green on the warm shores of the Black Sea. It is somewhat larger than West Virginia and almost twice as thickly settled, and it has had more feuds to the square mile, and bloodier ones, than West Virginia ever knew. For Georgia lay on the road between Europe and Asia, first stop on the long caravan route from the Mediterranean countries to the northern grasslands and faraway China. This made it a center of trade and of culture, but also a battleground.

They will tell you in Asia Minor that the Georgians are direct descendants of Noah, through Togarmah, grandson of Japheth, listed in Genesis 10:3. Scientists who study old ruins and manuscripts also say that the Georgians are very ancient. Three thousand years ago, when Rome had not been heard of and Homer of the Greeks had not been born, some tribes grew restless in Urartu, a long-forgotten kingdom in the lands where Armenia is now. This kingdom was always being invaded by Assyrians and Scythians, so these tribes moved to the southern slope of the Caucasus Mountains. They were the ancestors of the Georgians, and with their settlement just south of the world's second highest mountain range begins the story of the Georgian people in the tenth or eleventh century B.C.

They were a tall, slim people, courageous and handsome, with dark eyes and dark brown hair. They seem to have worshiped the sun and moon and planets and to have owned their property in "large families," as many as fifty or a hundred descendants under one old man. The old man was the head. They had a king and a powerful priesthood. They carried on their accustomed labors, raised food crops and grapes in the valleys, and pastured sheep and horses on the hills. Their artisans set up forges and made weapons and metal utensils, beautifully decorated and highly prized in all the eastern lands.

Here came the caravans from Iran and India, last stop on their way to the new Greek settlements; here came the Greeks, venturing east to Iran or north against the Scythians. Two high civilizations met in Georgia, the highest of the ancient world. They were the venerable civilization of Asia and the young civilization of Greece and later of Rome. The Georgians learned from both.

Georgians were more advanced than the Greeks in those

days. They knew how to smelt iron ore into metal and make iron utensils. This craft marks a great dividing line in history; on iron our modern world is based. The Greeks learned smelting of iron from the peoples of the Caucasus and the southeast shore of the Black Sea; these included Georgians and Armenians. The priests of the ancient Greek gods seem to have disapproved of the innovation. You remember the famous myth of Prometheus, the hero-man who stole the fire of the gods and turned it to men's uses and was chained forever to a cliff in the Caucasus as punishment. The story is not all fiction; most myths have some basis in fact.

The quest of the Golden Fleece is also not entirely legend. You remember the story—how Jason and his Argonauts sailed away to Colchis, seeking a golden fleece beyond the great sea. . . . Well, there really is a place named Colchis on the shores of the Black Sea in Georgia, and there are gold-bearing sands in those hills. Even today some men of the hills use the ancient method of panning gold. They wash the sands in a sheepskin and the bits of gold stick to the fleece. Then they burn the fleece and get gold from the ashes. So it seems that the Argonauts were a rather highhanded lot of gold prospectors, like those who went to the Klondike not many years ago.

The tribes who took up residence south of the Caucasus got a rich country for their children's children for the next three thousand years. But if they wanted peace they didn't get it. Their land was too attractive and convenient on the road between east and west. Georgia lay right on the route of the world conquerors. All the great wars between the strongest powers of the east and of the Mediterranean peoples passed over the Georgian land.

The Georgians themselves prized freedom; they never missed a chance to fight against any conqueror. So their history is a story of three thousand years of war. Even today when two men meet, the Georgian greeting is not "How do you do?" but "May victory attend thee," with the response "And thee also."

A nun named Nino converted Georgia to Christianity early in the fourth century A.D. Then the wars between Iran and Byzantium became colored with religion, for Byzantium was the headquarters of Christianity in the eastern world. The newly Christianized Georgians swung toward Byzantium; for a short time in the seventh century they fought themselves free from Iranian rule. Then the great Moslem crusades overwhelmed them; they came under the Arabian Empire. Georgia, with Armenia, became a Christian island in a great Moslem sea. So they have been for sixteen hundred years, down to the present day.

After the Arabian Empire fell, Georgia had a breathing spell of independence under its own kings. Its golden age flowered under Queen Tamara, in 1184–1212. It is odd to note how many golden ages have occurred under women rulers; the Elizabethan Age and the Victorian Era were the most remarkable periods that British history has known. But it seems especially noteworthy that the two most striking personalities of Georgia's long history were women: St. Nino, who gave the country its Christian religion, and Queen Tamara, who presided over its great renaissance of literature and art.

The hordes of Genghiz Khan swept into Georgia in the thirteenth century, burning the farms and cities and killing the people or taking them into slavery. Tamerlane overran the country and sacked it six times from end to end. When the failing power of Byzantium collapsed in 1453, Georgia lost its only Christian support and, side by side with Armenia, lay isolated among hostile Moslems. Turks and Iranians looted it in turn, separating it for five centuries from the civilization of our western world, which was rapidly progressing beyond the ancient east. The Georgian clergy sank into ignorance and immorality; Georgian nobles were demoralized by having to send their sons as hostages and their daughters as concubines to Iranians and Turks.

In the seventeenth and eighteenth centuries a new influence spread—that of Christian Russia on the north. For a brief time Georgia again won independence, but the constant invasions of Turks and Iranians caused the Georgian princes to ask the "protection" of the Russian tsar. Georgia became a Russian possession in 1801, and enjoyed a military security she had never had before. But step by step the tsar adopted a policy of "Russianizing" the land. Schools taught only in Russian; the use of the Georgian language was forbidden in business and in the law courts. The Georgian upper class even seemed to take pride in talking Russian and forgetting the heritage of its once-proud people, much as the Russian aristocracy during the same period took pride in adopting the language and manners of the French.

The people's love of freedom was not sleeping. Many uprisings of peasants against their Russian oppressors took place.

When modern industry began to develop in the nineties of the last century, the industrial workers began to organize trade unions. And it was the nineteen-year-old youth nicknamed "Soso" who led the first important strike in Georgia—that of the Tiflis railway shops in 1898.

The first World War laid heavy strain on Georgia. The men were away at the front and the fields went unworked. After the Russian Revolution of November, 1917, the entire Trans-Caucasus was a sort of no man's land for some three years. Turkish, German, and British armies seized the country in turn, lured by Baku's oil. Racial hates were incited into bitter conflicts; race and religious massacres took place. This period was

Georgia is the playground of the USSR—skiing on Mt. Elbrus—walking trips through ancient Svanetia

one of the hardest that Georgia has ever endured. Fortunately it was short; on February 25, 1921, as the Red Army approached from the north, Georgian workers revolted and seized power with its help.

Georgia became a Soviet state. For a time it was joined with Armenia and Azerbaidjan in a Trans-Caucasian Federation. In 1936 all three became separate sovereign states, constituent republics of the USSR.

It seems that there will never be an end to the great gray cliffs of the Caucasus and the cold mountain winds blowing between them. Then suddenly the towering snow peaks and cliffs disappear; the winds die away into stillness and all around the city of Tiflis are green farms, meadowland, vineyards, and orchards.

If you expected an Oriental city of dirt and disorder, you will be surprised by Tiflis. The best view of it is seen when going up the funicular railway. The roofs drop below, copper-colored in the sunlight. How precipitous and hilly the city is, with the Kura River twisting down its ravines! Just below are the famous sulphur baths from which the city was named, for Tiflis, also spelled Tbilisi, means "Warm Springs." It was founded in the fifth century and has been destroyed twenty-nine times during various invasions. You would never know it, to look at the wide asphalt streets and the tall apartment houses. Tiflis has almost doubled in size in the past ten years. It is today a city of more than half a million.

The Georgians are much better dressed than the people we have left behind in Russia. They seem to be interested in clothes, for they wear them jauntily with an air of pride. Tiflis is known as the Paris of the Orient. Women wear thin flowing silks and long scarves. They stroll languorously into shops that display fine wines and wonderful nougat candy. Many of the men wear the Georgian national costume—a well-fitting long coat, reaching to the knees, with a row of silvered cartridge cases on the breast, a neat cap of black karakul, smart baggy riding breeches decorated by a red stripe and stuck into soft black boots. Some sport revolvers on their hips and wear hand-hammered silver Georgian swords on dress occasions. In cool weather they add a long, flowing black cape of fuzzy felt known as a "burka." It makes them look very imposing on horseback and is practicable in the mountains as a combination blanket and tent.

The Georgians are warm-blooded and hospitable, full of the joy of life and much less serious in manner than the sober Russians. They take their visitors, not to see serious things like schools and factories, but to Georgian operettas, old castles, cool underground cafés. All good Georgian restaurants seem to be in cellars, with sawdust on the floor to "keep it clean." They offer you whole bottles of golden Georgian wine, and think it reflects on their hospitality if you fail to drink it all. The crowds at the tables will be very informal, singing gay songs and getting up occasionally to execute energetic dances with a short sword, with daggers, or with a fine handkerchief. They will take you to see the dawn over the river Kura. They will offer you trips to the south for no more serious reason than that "the spring has come there and the land is green." They may even urge you to "marry a Georgian and stay with us in Tiflis." Then they will brag of their country. And how they can brag!

You will learn that Georgia has all kinds of climate, from the very moist semitropical shores of the Black Sea to the cold winters and dry summers of the eastern valleys. Four million acres of forest lie on the slopes of the mountains, including a vast variety of trees and valuable woods used in airplane construc-

tion and the details of pianos and violins. Below the timber is
the zone of grain, with wheat in the drier east and corn in the
warm, moist west. Georgia is famous for vineyards; she supplies one-third of all the grapes in the USSR. Her wines go
abroad to the world market, where they challenge Burgundy. In
recent years special types of grapes have been produced for
champagne, which is made in a big factory in Tiflis.

The semitropical shores of the Black Sea are reserved for
crops like tea and citrus fruits. There are over 115,000 acres
of tea plantation, all publicly or cooperatively owned, and developed since the revolution. Georgian tea is beginning to drive
Indian and Chinese tea from the Russian market. There are
millions of orange trees and hundreds of thousands of lemon
trees; grapefruit also has been recently introduced. On the Black
Sea shores, surrounded by these orchards, lie a continuous suc-
cession of health resorts where people from all over the USSR
come for vacation, much as Americans go to California for its
warm sunny days.

Georgia has a valuable mineral, manganese, of special use in
making high-quality steel. Much of the world's known supply
of manganese is here in Georgian hills. Just before the second
World War they were producing 1,500,000 tons annually, four
times the output of tsarist years. It used to be mined in small
claims, wastefully; now the mines are modernized and mechanized. But the river still runs black from Chiaturi—black from
the refuse of the manganese.

The Georgians are proud of the factories of Tiflis. The old
railway shops where Stalin organized the first strike have been
greatly expanded, but these are now dwarfed by much larger
enterprises: the steel mill which supplies iron and steel to all
Trans-Caucasia, the machine-building plant making machines
for the Baku oil industry, a shoe factory which is one of the

Citrus fruits abound in Georgia and tea-pickers find a rich harvest

The Children's Railroad in Tiflis—built and operated by children

Soviet Union's largest, a plant that makes textile machinery for the entire silk industry of the USSR.

"The national income of Georgia," they will tell you, "is about twenty times what it was in tsarist days."

They are also proud of the children's railway, built some years ago by the children of the railway workers. It is a regular railway several miles long, with small but real locomotives and cars on which children ride. It has a station, sells tickets and collects them, and uses the "profits" to "extend the road." Everything is done by the youngsters, who thus learn railroading as a game. There are many such children's railroads in the Soviet Union, but they all copied Tiflis. The Georgians were first.

The Georgians are a well-educated people. The language they read and write is one of the puzzles of the Sphinx; it consists of queer curlicues and no scholar has yet decided where it came from. Today the Georgians have compulsory education; they have over 700,000 pupils in grade schools and secondary schools, five times as many as in 1914. They have 18 universities with 22,000 students. They have a branch of the Academy of Sciences. Their theaters would attract attention anywhere in the world.

Moscow went wild when the Rustaveli Theater came to the All-Union Olympiad of National Theaters in 1930. The stage was filled from floor to ceiling with colorful dramatic motion. Georgian actors seldom took two steps on a level. They would leap up six feet of mountain crags just to emphasize a sentence. The scenery seemed made to give them crags up which to leap. The director explained that the graceful, powerful movement was the natural Georgian gait developed by the mountain life and the national costume.

No one who saw it will ever forget a scene that was played on fourteen different levels—the flat roofs of a village on a steep hill. The girls came out on the roofs to welcome their men back from a victory. Then girls and men together danced on the roofs, the women tossing bright silken shawls of many colors while the men threw great black burkas through the air, stamping their feet in the joy of victorious return. This was only one of a dozen brilliant scenes that caused both Russian and foreign critics to hail the Rustaveli Theater as worthy of world renown.

The old hates of the Caucasus seem to have disappeared entirely, as far as the peoples within the Soviet Union are concerned. The Georgians, Azerbaidjanians, and Armenians compete today in drama, in farm and factory records, instead of in war.

But the Georgians like to be asked "Don't you object to being under the Russians?" because they have such a good reply.

"Under the Russians?" they answer loftily. "Oh, no, we're not. Our Soso sits in the Kremlin. The Russians are under us!"

ARMENIA, THE EARLIEST CHRISTIAN STATE

MOST OF US have met Armenians. They are a very ancient people who live at the eastern end of Asia Minor, south of the Caucasus Mountains. They are proud of their long history. They are proudest of all to remember that they were the earliest Christian state in the world, holding their religion firmly through centuries of persecution by the fire-worshiping Iranians and later by the Moslem Turks. Their land has been split under alien rulers; their people have been refugees all over the world. Today they possess a small but cherished country, one of the sovereign states of the USSR.

Soviet Armenia is not a large country. You could drop two Armenias into Lake Superior and have a lake the size of Ontario left. However, Armenia is as big as Belgium and its civilization is much more ancient. It has 11,580 square miles and probably close to 1,500,000 people, for its population has grown very fast in recent years.

Erevan, the capital of Armenia, is only an hour and a half by plane from Tiflis, chief junction for republics south of the Caucasus. The plane flies due south, keeping high in the air to avoid the mountains. Below it runs a railway line and the yellow ribbons of winding roads among wooded hills. The tilled fields around little hamlets reach almost to the wooded summits. It is clear that the people here are industrious, working every bit of their land. Here and there we see old fortresses and medieval monasteries and ruins of ancient towns. It is clear that people have worked in this land for many centuries.

Off to the left a great mountain lake gleams in the sunlight; it is Lake Sevan, one of the largest mountain lakes in the world. The mountains grow higher among the peaks of the Little Caucasus. The sun falls on snowy summits and on dark green mountain meadows where large flocks are pasturing. Suddenly the mountains are cut by a grayish yellow plain watered by a river. Just beyond it stands the highest mountain of all, rising alone out of the plain in impressive majesty. It is Ararat, covered with eternal snow. This is the peak on which the ark of Noah was said to have landed.

At Erevan the peak of Ararat towers above the city against the bright blue sky. Wherever you go in Armenia you can see this mountain. Ararat is the symbol of Armenia; in ancient days it gave its name to a kingdom which was called "Urartu" (Ararat) by the Assyrians. In modern days it is also a symbol of Armenia's fate. This beloved mountain is not today owned by the Armenians; it lies just across the Arax River in Turkey. The Turks once protested to Moscow because Armenians used on their coat of arms a mountain that belonged to Turkey. The Russians answered: "Turkey's national emblem is the crescent. Does Turkey thereby claim the moon?"

The oldest indication of human beings in this region is a skeleton that was found under twenty feet of earth when the Armenians dug foundations for their new power station in 1925. A flint implement with the skeleton shows that the man belonged to the early Stone Age; there is no way of knowing how many thousands of years ago he lived. There are many relics of the later Stone Age which show that a considerable number of people lived here as early as 3000 B.C. They had a well-developed irrigation system and an odd alphabet that has only recently been deciphered. They appear to have worshiped the goddess of water.

The people of Urartu seem to have been progressive. They kept up with new discoveries. When human beings discovered the use of bronze, Urartu had fine bronze workers. When iron came into use they had skillful ironworkers. The great iron mines of the ancient world lay on the southern shores of the Black Sea west of Ararat. A king of Urartu named Menuas built a forty-six-mile canal some 2740 years ago that is still used for irrigation.

The first mention of the modern name Armenia was in an inscription by the Persian king Darius about 521 B.C. A new race of people seems to have arrived from Europe a little before that time, a tall slim people with long narrow faces, light brown complexion, and soft dark hair. They mixed with the people of Urartu to make the modern race with the new name. Armenians were thus an energetic, prosperous people long before the rise of Greece and Rome. When Greek civilization became the standard of progress, the Armenian upper circles spoke Greek and sent their boys to Athens to finish their education. When the Roman Empire arose, Armenian boys studied in Rome. The Armenians fought for their country's independence against Rome's best commanders, inflicting on them some serious defeats. Rome finally conquered them in 72 B.C.

An Armenian king made Christianity the state religion in A.D. 280, forty years before the emperor Constantine made it the religion of the Roman Empire. By the Armenian king's order all the property of the pagan temples was given to the Christian Church, which thus became the most powerful landlord in the country—owning 12,000 farms and able to raise an army of both infantry and cavalry from the serf peasants who worked its lands. A monk made a new alphabet, for the Armenians could no longer read the alphabet of their ancient inscriptions. A "modern" Armenian literature began, consisting mostly of religious works.

In those days the discussions of the learned men were chiefly about religion. People fought and died for slight differences of theology. Armenians are stubborn people; their bishops soon disagreed with the theology of the bishops outside Armenia. The Armenian Church has maintained its own form of Christianity since about A.D. 400, never submitting its views either to the head of the Greek Church or to the Pope of Rome.

Armenians suffered bitterly for their religion. The Persians conquered them as Rome declined. To Armenians their religion was a symbol of independence; to the Persian king it was a symbol of treason to his rule. Terrible massacres of Christians took place. One Persian king gathered thousands of Armenians together and had them trampled to death by elephants.

The rising power of the Ottoman Turks conquered Constantinople in 1453; they then waged war with ancient Iran. These two great powers fought over Armenia and held it in turn. The Russian Empire spread southward and reached the

Caucasus in the eighteenth century. The Armenians, like the Georgians, appealed to Christian Russia for aid. After severe war, part of Armenia was joined to Russia early in the nineteenth century; but part remained under the Turks. This led to continuous friction; the unhappy Armenians have suffered from all the pressures of world politics for the past century and a half.

Those Armenians who came under Russia were at first happy in having Christian rule. But the Russian Church persecuted the Armenian Church as unorthodox; from 1836 onward all teaching in the Armenian language was forbidden, in the tsar's effort to Russianize the land. The persecutions in Turkish Armenia were so much worse that Armenians often begged Russia to take the rest of Armenia from the Turks. The worst of all the slaughters came during the first World War—in which Turks and Russians were on different sides, so that all Armenians were considered traitors by the Turks.

In the summer of 1915 in all of Turkish Armenia the people were driven from their towns and villages on the "march of death." Old men, women, and children were sent through the mountains into the Arabian deserts. Nothing was done to keep them alive on the way or at their destination. The Turkish government telegraphed its German ally that it had decided to "solve the Armenian problem by exterminating the Armenian race." Of one city of 18,000 only 350 were left alive; from another city of 19,000 only 11 survived. Four years later the report of Dr. Fridtjof Nansen to the League of Nations on Armenian relief stated that of 1,845,450 Armenians who had formerly lived in Turkey 1,000,000 were dead and more than 600,000 were scattered to the ends of earth.

The Turks had "settled" their Armenian problem; there were only some 200,000 Armenians left in Turkey. The Turks had incidentally taken Armenian property valued at billions of dollars. They had set the precedent later followed by Hitler against the Jews. The League of Nations passed good resolutions about giving the Armenians a "national home independent of Ottoman rule." But no one was willing to give additional territory to Soviet Russia and no one was willing to supply the army necessary to hold a small separate Armenia against the Turks. The League tried to get rid of Armenia by offering it to America; President Wilson wisely declined.

The Armenians suffered not only from Turkey. In the last stage of the World War, Germany, Great Britain, France, and Turkey sent troops into the Caucasus in a race for Baku oil. They subsidized various local governments, including one in Armenia. Under these pressures bitter race wars broke out all over Trans-Caucasia. At the end of 1920 a Soviet government was set up in what had been Russian Armenia, while Turkish Armenia—with its people dead or driven out—remained under Turkey.

By all these wars and massacres one-third of the Armenian people were destroyed in less than five years. Another third were scattered all over the world. Thousands of them carried their knowledge of irrigated farming into America's irrigated valleys; others exploit in the cities the proud craft of rug weaving that goes back thirty centuries. Turkey has an uneasy conscience about its border with the USSR, fearing lest someday Soviet Armenia may want the Armenian lands now held by the Turks.

Armenian writers wrote for many centuries in a classic tongue that the common people could not understand. About a hundred years ago Abovian's famous novel *The Wounds of Armenia*, written in the everyday language, started a new fashion in literature. Abovian's statue stands today in front of the Erevan Opera House—a thin youthful figure in a student's cloak, with modest poetic face. The opera house is new, one of the finest in the USSR.

The Erevan that Abovian knew remained almost unchanged until the first World War. It was a little town of 30,000 people who lived in flat-roofed clay houses on narrow alleys, dusty in summer and muddy in winter. Blacksmiths were shoeing horses and oxen in the main street; the barber shaved customers under a spreading tree in the market place. Caravans of camels plodded slowly under the high gate of the caravanserai, a romantic word that means only a "barn for a caravan." There were just four industrial establishments in the city: a cognac distillery, a cannery, a small power plant, and a cotton gin. If you add the brewery in a near-by city and a small copper smelter in the hills, you have the sum total of Armenian industry as late as 1913.

Abovian would not recognize his Erevan if he came back to it now. It is a lively city of 200,000 people with many apartment houses on wide paved streets. Much of the city has a soft reddish color, for it is built of a colored rock quarried in Armenian hills. Government buildings are ornamented with Armenian marble. We would not mention the streetcars, autobusses, water and sewage system, for every American takes these for granted; but Erevan had none of these in pre-Soviet days.

The dreary little suburb of clay houses that Abovian knew behind the market place is now the industrial district with many new apartment houses, clubs, and restaurants clustering around big new industries. The biggest is the synthetic rubberworks making rubber out of limestone by a complicated process that needs plenty of cheap electric power. Armenia has endless quantities of limestone and an almost endless source of power from the Zanga River cascades. So Erevan expects to be the rubber capital of the USSR.

The cellars of Ararat Wine Trust offer a taste of their cognac; it is marketed abroad and is considered much better than Greek or Italian liquor. The old distillery had a hundred workers, but the publicly owned Ararat Wine Trust employs several thousand. The old cannery has been replaced by a great new cannery entered through a garden of roses and carnations; it put out 17,000,000 cans of fruit in 1939. Erevan preserves of rose petals and nuts are known in faraway northern lands. The famous rug weaving continues but not in the dim mud huts; the weavers have a large cooperative enterprise in well-lighted modern buildings. With all these improvements it is not so surprising that the output of Armenian industry in 1937 was fourteen times that of 1913.

Farming also has been modernized. In old Armenia the peasants used crooked wooden plows and reaped with sickles; few farmers had a metal plow. Modern Armenia had 1500

Wine barrels at the Erevan Wine and Cognac plant—one of twelve such mechanized plants now operating in Armenia

tractors in 1938; three-fourths of its farmwork is done by machinery. The crop area—over 1,000,000 acres—is five times that of the black days of 1919.

Hundreds of miles of road have been built to connect the farms with the cities. Many places are still unreached by road, where high mountains shut in tiny hamlets. A tourist might think he was still in Bible times. But here are new houses, schools, and clinics, and the oldest mud house, whose outside looks as it did in the days of Alexander of Macedon, is very different inside. Clocks are ticking, sewing machines humming, books lying about, and electric light from a new power plant falls on new furniture bought with the increased harvests.

Armenia has a source of tremendous energy in the Zanga River, which drops rapidly from Lake Sevan to Erevan—falling 3281 feet within sixty miles. Three power plants have been built on the Zanga cascades as part of a plan to harness the entire river with nine plants.

There is a fourth electric power station, which belongs to the children of Erevan. It is set in the Children's Park on the river. It has only forty kilowatts of energy; but it is a regular station, with which the children light their theater, motion-picture house, dining room, and bathing beach. Different groups of children take turns, so that all may learn to handle electricity. This station also serves the children's railroad, which was copied from the one in Tiflis. A marble staircase, ornamented with flowers and plants, leads into the railway station, from which operates a train of three cars accommodating 150 small passengers.

Armenians are proud of their modern country, but they do not forget their long past. A little way out of Erevan stands the oldest building in the USSR that is still in use. It is a cathedral built in A.D. 303 and preserved entire to the present

Armenia boasts a rich cotton crop and is fast developing an important silk industry

day. Architects admire the perfect relation between its form and material and its purpose. Today it is a museum of ancient Armenian manuscripts. These are important not only to Armenians but to the world, for some writings of famous Greek and Roman authors have come down to us only in Armenian translations.

Here in glass cases lie rare books written by learned men of past centuries, ornamented in colors on parchment or rough bluish paper. There are tiny books no bigger than a pocket matchbox and giant volumes weighing seventy-five pounds. The manuscripts of the tenth and eleventh centuries show colors as fresh as if painted yesterday. Here are recorded the thoughts of poets, historians, saints, and mathematicians whose prayers and struggles helped build a nation lasting through all the years.

In the bad days of 1919 the population of Armenia dropped to 722,000, but it rose to 1,281,000 in 1939 and is probably 1,500,000 today. Today's Armenia is educated. Schools opened rapidly after the revolution; by 1939 over 400,000 children and grownups were studying, about one-third of all the people.

An old man named Asatran came back to Armenia. He had worked for thirty years in the vineyards of France. In his old age he sold his modest possessions and took with him only vines that he had developed and from which excellent dessert wine could be made. All the way to Armenia he carefully preserved these vines as his gift to his motherland. When he reached Soviet Armenia he found that in his long absence his country had developed better grapes.

Old Asatran was at first quite brokenhearted. "They don't need me any more," he mourned. The Armenian gardeners reassured him. His vines, it is true, were not greatly needed. But he himself was needed for the qualities that Armenia has prized for thirty centuries and that the new Armenia even more greatly honors—the skill and handicraft developed through a life of careful toil.

Today's Armenia knows that peaceful toil must be defended. Bitter experience has taught it what Hitler's destruction of "inferior races" means. There have been many Armenian heroes and heroines in the second World War. An eighteen-year-old Armenian girl named Asya won three military decorations for her work as a nurse under fire at Stalingrad, carrying wounded men from the field.

There are thirty Armenian generals in the Red Army. One of them is Bagramyan, famed in the lifting of the siege of Leningrad.

In the grim days when the Germans reached the Caucasus Mountains a young Armenian, gay, black-haired Mesrop, volunteered to blow up a strategic bridge. He heard a German sentry coming. There was no time to set a long fuse and escape. So he set a short fuse and blew up the bridge, the sentry, and himself. A Red Army soldier picked up a water flask floating down the river; in it were Mesrop's last words: "Good-by, my sunny Armenian land, my parents, and my fighting comrades. Victory will be ours. Remember your comrade Mesrop."

AZERBAIDJAN, BRIDE OF FIRE

THE TALE OF A VERY ancient fight for freedom became the
theme of a modern drama at the Moscow Olympiad of National
Theaters in 1930. It was called *The Bride of Fire*. It brought
before the world a long-forgotten story.

A thousand years ago the serfs of the Baku oil region
rebelled against the fire-worshiping Iranian kings. Three
powers were fighting one another: the ancient Zoroastrians,
worshiping fire by human sacrifice; the Moslems, advancing
from Arabia; the local lords, scheming for their own rule.
Against this triple oppression rose Il Han, a serf. In hope of
luring him from the people's fight, the rulers offered him a
famous beauty—the "bride of fire." Il Han rejected the
maiden and died fighting for freedom.

For a thousand years the name of Il Han seemed forgotten. Somewhere in the people's memory it remained. When Azerbaidjan became a Soviet Republic, its people brought out this bit of their past. An author wrote a play about it for their national theater. It was a new theater, for the Moslem religion forbids dramatic art; only after the revolution of 1917 did young folks of Azerbaidjan act in plays. When they were invited to the Olympiad in Moscow, they displayed the heroic past of their people in this drama *The Bride of Fire.*

It was a good choice as a symbol of Azerbaidjan. Here lies, at Baku, the richest oil field in the world. Many wars for this oil have made the very earth flame from fires kindled in the seepages. The struggles of great and alien powers have burned up the lives of the humble people who live in this oil-bearing land.

Quite possibly the ancient fire worship of Zoroaster began in this region. The prophet himself is said to have been born on the lower Arax, which joins the Kura River here to enter the Caspian Sea. In the eighth century B.C. he came to Iran "from the northern mountains"; such mountains lie between Iran and Azerbaidjan today. The fires that break out with terrific power in oil fields may have inspired his religion. In any case the "eternal fire" of the Zoroastrians burned for many centuries on a high tower in Baku.

The ancient Greeks knew this land as "Caspiana." The Arabs called it "Agvan." The people in it call themselves Azerbaidjanians. They came into this country centuries ago from the grasslands of the nomads. They are related both to the people of Turkey and to the peoples of Central Asia. All are called Turkic and Turco-Tatar peoples.

"Pleasant and fair is the land of Agvan," an Arab writer declared in the tenth century. "The fields are rich in grain, vines, cotton, silk, salt, and oil. . . . The great Kura River brings fish in abundance." This variety of products is found in Azerbaidjan today. It is a land full of contrasts, from the bleak glaciers and green pastures of the mountains to the jungles and swamps of the lowlands and the dry parched valleys by the Caspian Sea. It supplies salt to all the peoples of the Caucasus. It grows rice, cotton, and many fruits. But its world fame comes from its great city, Baku.

Azerbaidjan is less than half the size of Utah but has six times as many people. Its area is 33,200 square miles, its population about 3,000,000 This large population is due to the Baku region. There are over 800,000 people in Baku alone. After Moscow and Leningrad it is one of the largest cities of the USSR.

It is nearly three days by rail from Moscow to the oil capital. The train travels due south for a day and a half through the Ukraine, then swings far east around the Caucasus Mountains and south again by the Caspian Sea. Here the mountains break off sharply at the "gates of Derbent," an ancient passage for tribes migrating into Europe from Central Asia. The passage is narrow. The water gleams blue on our left, while the cliffs rise steeply on our right. Beyond this point we are already in Asia, in the Azerbaidjan Republic. It is only a short distance now to Baku.

The ruins of the old khan's castle still stand on the hill above Baku. The city has centuries of history behind it. However, it remained a small place until the sixties of the last century—a dusty settlement of 13,000 people, swept by great sandstorms, a most unpleasant place in which to live. Russians came here not for pleasure but for easy money. The kerosene that Russia could buy from the United States dwindled in quantity because of the American Civil War. Companies were formed and wells were drilled in feverish haste.

The Nizami Square in Baku, oil capital of the USSR

Within twenty years Baku's oil output surpassed that of the United States. In 1901 Baku reached 11,000,000 metric tons, half the world output. Baku was oil capital of the world!

Forests of black shiny derricks arose against every horizon, against blue skies or blue water or in the smoky hollows of hills. A hundred streams of machine oils, green and brown and golden, poured day and night, winter and summer, in the oil refineries. The power plant was larger than any in Europe.

In all of this fabulously rich region there were no flowers or even bushes. The mocking blue of the Caspian is salt, nourishing no vegetation. The climate is arid with very little rain. The soil is so salty that even when rain falls on it a thin crust is formed through which green shoots cannot push. The only trees anywhere near Baku in those days were in the Villa Petrolla, a group of four good houses built for the engineers of the biggest oil company. They were later used by the Soviet government for a children's home.

Nobody asked Baku to produce beauty. It was asked only to produce oil. All the wealth went far away from Baku. It went to Petersburg, to London, to Paris, and to New York. The workers in the oil fields were mostly Azerbaidjanians under Russian engineers. The workers could neither read nor write. They could drill oil wells. As time went on they learned to drill with rotary oil drills fresh from America.

Despite the new machinery the oil output declined. The fields were wastefully managed. There were 153 different oil companies, each of which had dozens of small claims. Each company bored wells around the edges of its land in order to drain the oil from its neighbor's claims. The greatest problem was the water which seeped underground from the Caspian into the wells. Each company tried to shift the floods to its neighbors. The oil engineers knew that such methods were wasteful, but in those days of competition it seemed that nothing else could be done.

The Russians lived in White Town; but the local workers lived in Black Town, which got its name because it was so black and greasy with oil. Up the narrow streets the Moslem women toiled, drawing their veils across their faces with one hand and balancing heavy water buckets on their heads with the other. There were no streetcars or autobusses; so, as the oil fields spread, the workers moved out to live among the derricks in huts of gray stone or yellow clay.

One of these huts has been kept as a museum. It is of hard clay and rises only five feet above the earth. Instead of a door, there is a narrow chink covered with a board. Instead of windows, there is one small hole in the wall just under the clay roof.

There is no grass or green plant anywhere around, but only gray dust stained with dark greasy oil. Nobody now would believe that people could live in such a place.

The oilworkers at Baku were naturally discontented. Baku became the chief center of the Bolshevik Party for all of southeastern Russia from 1905 onward. The largest printing plant for forbidden revolutionary literature in all of tsarist Russia was hidden in Baku. Stalin worked there together with many people who are high in the Soviet government today.

When the Baku oilworkers heard by telegram in 1917 that the Petersburg government was in the hands of the Bolsheviks, they took over the city government and declared the oil of Baku the property of the people. They had little trouble at first, for the private owners were thousands of miles away. Most of the lands belonged to the Russian tsar. The owners next in line were the corporations who leased from the tsar the right to operate wells. Their shares of stock were in London or Paris or New York, separated from Baku by a thousand miles of war. Most of the local managers were Russian engineers; they kept right on with their work. The engineers knew that the old ways of work were wasteful and, since they now belonged to a single owner, the wells were organized into eight great districts with one central management.

It seemed very simple to most of the people of Baku, but it started a panic in oil shares in the stock markets of the world. The great nations at once began a race for Baku oil. The Germans and the Turks came from the north and west. The British came up from Iran. Each big power backed some local group through which it hoped to get the oil. All of this stirred up the ancient hates of the peoples of the Caucasus.

The years of war ruined the oil fields. They had almost ceased producing. The salt water of the Caspian had seeped into the neglected wells until nine-tenths of the liquid taken out was water. The new Soviet government had no money for repairs and new machinery. No loans could be had from abroad, where Baku oil was bitterly discussed in all the conferences of big nations that were settling the problems of Europe.

The Soviet oil engineers drew up a plan to rebuild the oil fields from the sale of oil. The oilworkers' trade unions agreed to work very hard for many years for little pay. Oil was shipped into Russia and also to foreign countries. Every cent was used to buy machinery from America and to reorganize the oil industry on a modern base. Oil was one of the first branches of the publicly owned industries of the USSR to advance. The output increased very slowly at first and then, with the new machinery, rapidly went ahead.

The changes in the life of Baku for the past fifty years are mirrored in the oil output. Oil production in America expanded, while Baku's declined to 7,700,000 tons in 1913. In 1920 after the wars destroyed the wells, the oil output was only 2,500,000 tons. After twelve years of rebuilding, it reached 12,000,000 tons—higher than its greatest previous peak. In five more years the output doubled, reaching 23,900,000 tons in 1938. It continued to rise during the second World War.

As the oil industry prospered, Baku became a modern city. A wide boulevard runs for many miles beside the blue-green sea. From it lead busy streets with streetcars and autobusses, and broad avenues lined with apartment houses and even with trees. An electric interurban connects the city with the oil fields; it was built in 1926, the first electric railway in the USSR. There are two water systems, one from underground rivers and the other from the mountains a hundred miles away. Other industries have arisen, including a textile factory weaving 40,-000,000 yards of cotton goods annually and a shoe factory making each year 500,000 pairs of shoes.

The rice terraces of Lenkoran

Azerbadjanian school children   A parachutist with her grandmother

Baku oil was the prize for which the German armies drove into the lands of the Caucasus, to their great defeat at Stalingrad.

Baku has been important to the United Nations in the second World War, not only for the oil supplied to the Red Army but as first stop for American lend-lease supplies coming into the Soviet Union through Iran. American and British diplomats and correspondents, who could no longer reach the USSR directly across Europe, flew by Africa to Teheran, capital of Iran, and then by short hop northward over the mountains to Baku. When Stalin flew south to the famous Teheran conference with President Roosevelt and Prime Minister Churchill, his last stop in the USSR was Baku.

Twenty years ago farmers in Azerbaidjan, like other farmers in the Caucasus, plowed with heavy wooden plows drawn by oxen. Today they use more than 4000 tractors. Two farming regions are especially interesting because of the problems they present.

In the mountains between Armenia and Azerbaidjan are many pastures used by both peoples. Terrible cattle plagues often broke out when the herdsmen went to the high pastures. Herdsmen fought to the death with other herdsmen, accusing them of bringing the plague. These conflicts were increased by race prejudice between the Moslem Azerbaidjanians and the Christian Armenians. In some of these mountain areas only one-third of the people were left alive after the race wars of 1919. Today these conflicts have ceased, not only because each people has its own republic but because the pastures are controlled by experienced veterinaries who enforce quarantine. These specialists are the honored rulers of the pastures.

At the southern tip of Azerbaidjan is a low-lying jungle called Lenkoran. It is a dream region for exploring botanists.

Tigers and leopards prowl among prehistoric varieties of trees. The farmers here grow golden figs, blood-red pomegranates, and rice. They harness the terrible-looking Indian zebus for plowing.

Rice growing is not a healthy occupation. Rice loves water; it is grown in artificially made swamps. Clouds of mosquitoes carry malaria. People work all day standing in mud and water. This is how rice growers live all over the east, in India, Japan, and China. Thus also they once lived in Lenkoran. The cemeteries were bigger than the villages. There were graves of children who never grew up; there were graves of peasant rice growers, almost none of whom lived more than forty years.

The Soviet government of Azerbaidjan debated the question. "If we stop rice growing it will be easier to fight malaria, but Lenkoran will remain poor. If we increase rice fields and make Lenkoran rich, the danger of malaria will increase. Which shall we choose, rice or health?" They decided to choose both. So they put their scientists, doctors, and airplane pilots to work.

Today a new white building topped with a red crescent stands in every third or fourth village of Lenkoran. It is the malaria station of the Red Crescent, the Moslem form of Red Cross. This station watches the flooding, which is done at intervals fixed by the scientists. Oil from Baku is poured on the extra swamps where rice is not planted. Other chemicals are dusted into the rice swamps to kill the larvae of mosquitoes. Lenkoran has its rice crops, and malaria is being brought under control.

In former days the only schools in Azerbaidjan were in the Russian language, which most of the children in the country could not understand. In 1914 there were 72,000 children in school, many of them from families of Russian engineers and officials. Teaching today is carried on in whatever language the children speak. In Azerbaidjan there are fifteen different languages and there are schools in all of these languages. This is expensive, but it is necessary so that every child can have an education. There were 582,000 children in school in 1937, eight times as many as in 1914.

Before the revolution there was not a single institution of higher learning in Azerbaidjan; today there are sixteen. There are also twenty research institutes and ninety-three technical schools. Formerly there were only twelve oil engineers of native birth; now there are more than 3000.

Women went veiled among these people twenty years ago. Today they are unveiled and participate in public life. There are 5000 women students in the universities. The richest oil field in the USSR is managed by a woman, who is also a member of the government of Azerbaidjan. The chiefs of the health and social-welfare departments of the Azerbaidjan Republic are women.

Once the oil of Baku brought wars. Great gushers went up in flames, burning many villages. Azerbaidjan was a "bride of fire." But, as Zoroaster taught, fire can be either good or evil, as it is controlled. Today Azerbaidjan has made of her rich oil field the husband who supports her house.

KAZAKHS, PEOPLE OF THE NAMELESS PLAINS

DURING THE SECOND WORLD WAR an exhibition was held in Alma Ata—a city far in Asia at the foot of the Tien Shan Mountains, last stopping place in the USSR on the airplane route to China. The exhibits displayed the progress of science in Kazakhstan, of which Alma Ata is the capital. People stared at a model showing the practice of witch doctors just twenty years ago.

The favorite "cure" consisted in wrapping the sick man in the bloody skin of a freshly killed lamb—the meat of the lamb went to the witch doctor—seating him on red-hot stones and flogging him until he fainted. When the patient lost consciousness the witch doctor rejoiced that the "evil spirit is leaving." This was shown in the exhibition side by side with the pictures of hundreds of hospitals, health resorts, and research institutions of modern Kazakhstan.

The Kazakhs are proud of their progress. They are proud of their great republic. It is the biggest republic in the USSR except for the Russian Republic. It is more than 1,000,000 square miles in extent, a third as large as the United States of America. It especially resembles the great plains and deserts of the American southwest and, like them, is sparsely settled, having only some 6,000,000 people.

"Ours is the land that has everything," the Kazakhs tell you, "wheat, cotton, livestock, every kind of mineral. We reach from the Ural Mountains to China, from the blue Caspian Sea to the snows of the Siberian Altai. Half of our land is considered desert, but our Academy of Sciences is exploring it. We have already discovered in this so-called useless desert 240 million acres of land capable of being tilled. Our Ural-Emba oil deposits are the largest in the Union, probably the largest in the world. In copper we are first in the Union. We have tremendous deposits of other minerals. The only thing we are short of is people. We need many times our present population to develop the vast riches of our land."

Since the Kazakhs have more land than they can develop, they invite settlers to come from European Russia and especially from the crowded parts of the Ukraine. They pride themselves on their hospitality to new settlers; hospitality has been honored among Kazakhs for centuries. Today they lay out farms and build homes and then invite the settlers. The farmers of the Ukraine send delegates to inspect the various possibilities and to choose their future home. They come in large groups and form a whole new village.

Twenty-five years ago this Kazakhstan, now so proud of it-

Kazakh farmers hunt game in the Soviet Tien-Shan Mountains; other
Kazakhs, living on the endless plains, mine for valuable minerals

self, was a land that had lost its name. The Russians conquered it gradually during the eighteenth and nineteenth centuries; it was the first territory they owned in Asia south of Siberia. The Russians did not trouble to learn the name of the people. They called all dark-skinned people "natives" and split their land into Russian provinces. Only after the revolution, when the native peoples began to express themselves, was it discovered that the Kazakhs were a nation with a language and a past.

In the fifteenth century they were already roving this area, a nomad people under a powerful khan. They seem to have been a mixed race related to the Mongols but with a Turkish language. When Russians from Siberia penetrated the land in the sixteenth century, three Kazakh "hordes" under different chieftains united for mutual protection against the tribes of Mongolia and Chinese Turkestan. Fear of these eastern enemies led the tribal leaders of all the Kazakhs, meeting in 1738 at the Russian military post of Orenburg—on the border between Europe and Asia—to accept voluntarily the "protection" of the Russian tsar.

Russian armed forces set up forts in Kazakh territory. Russian settlers took the best of the Kazakhs' lands, 100 million acres of good soil. Russian law from 1747 onward made it a crime to sell arms or ammunition to "natives"; so the Kazakhs, who from time to time rose up against their Russian overlords, were always easily put down. The last and greatest uprising was the rebellion of 1916, in which all the native peoples of Central Asia participated. It took the tsar's troops seven months—from July, 1916, to January, 1917—to crush this rebellion. Tens of thousands of Kazakhs were slain; 300,000 fled into China, returning in 1918 in the early days of Soviet rule.

The new Soviet government did not even know the name of all the native peoples. They called all migratory herdsmen

"Kirghiz" at first. As soon as the herdsmen understood that they had self-government they declared that they were different peoples—that the Kirghiz were people of the mountain pastures, while the Kazakhs were people of the great plains. Then the lands of the Kazakhs were separated from those of the Kirghiz and the nameless plains were named. In 1920 Kazakhstan became an autonomous republic under Russia. In 1936 it had grown in wealth and education to the point where it became one of the sovereign republics of the USSR. These once-nameless folk were then found to possess the second largest of all the Soviet Republics.

The Kazakhs have many legends about horses. There was a famous horse named Konur-At who died of thirst in the desert. Modern Kazakhs speak of the coming of the "great iron horse" who conquered the desert forever for all the Kazakh people. They mean the Turkestan-Siberian Railway, the great north-south line across Asia, the first "giant" of the Five Year Plan to be completed on May 1, 1930. Today in the desert, where the legendary horse Konur-At perished, stands a flourishing copper town reached by rail. It is Kounrad, named for the horse.

At Aina-Bulak, a once-empty spot in the plains, representatives of many Soviet nations, amid cheers from the mighty gathering, added their blows to drive the final spike at the opening of the "Turk-Sib Railway." This spike united Siberia with Central Asia. It changed forever the life of half a continent. It joined two streams of life—the one along the forest rivers of Siberia and the caravan life of the southern plains. The center of this new united life is Kazakhstan.

Friendship and equality of Russians and Kazakhs was the keynote of the celebration. Open-air theaters gave performances in both languages. Football teams of Siberia and Turkmenia contended till dusk. An enormous crane that went by the name of

"Marion"—its painted inscription said that it came from Marion, Ohio—lifted human beings in its bucket, always a Russian and a Kazakh together, and swung them fifty feet in air amid cheers.

The wild Kazakh horsemen had a race of their own across a great valley. They rode madly, so drunken with speed that they almost rode down several persons—including Isaief, President of Kazakhstan. The younger Kazakhs sat along the rails, patting the iron with pride and chanting old songs with new words. They were already employed on the railroad and attending the railroad schools. They sang of the evil past when "they stole even our name, calling us Kirghiz." They sang of the "black-iron steed, swifter than a hundred horses," that belonged to no chieftain or trader but to all the Kazakh people.

After the railroad came, Kazakhstan developed rapidly. In a few years the cattle more than doubled—in 1932 there were 4,500,000 head of cattle; in 1939 there were 10,000,000. But cattle herding ceased to be the main occupation. All over Kazakhstan the once-migrant herdsmen began to settle to the soil.

Bitter fights went on between the old men and the young folks. The old men declared: "For thousands of years our people were free rovers; you shame your ancestors by forsaking their ways." The young folks studied, took up farming and industry. They abandoned the "yurts" for frame houses, built with timber brought by the railway from Siberian woods. Settled villages grew so fast that there were not enough names for them; they were called "Village Number One . . ." "Number Seven . . ." "Number Forty."

The desert began to retreat. The dry plains proved suitable for modern power farming. By 1939, 25,000 tractors and thousands of harvester combines were tilling the soil and har-

A new motion picture theatre in Alma Ata

Two Kazakhs inspect the wonders of a switch on the "Turk-Sib" railroad

vesting the wheat. Irrigation was carried on wherever there was a river. Thousands of acres in a region called the "Hungry Steppe" were tamed to produce cotton.

All over Kazakhstan was heard the tapping of the geologist's hammer. New cities arose to develop newly found mineral deposits. Emba became a great oil center; Aktiubinsk became a chemical city, turning beds of phosphorite into fertilizer. In the empty desert arose Karaganda, a city of 160,000, the center of the third largest coal region of the USSR. The meat-packing plant in Semipalatinsk grew to the size of the big packing plants of Chicago.

One discovery made in Kazakhstan was to prove of strategic importance in the second World War. Rubber-bearing bushes were found growing wild on the dry plains; they are "kok-sagyz" and "tau-sagyz." Most of the world's natural rubber comes from the tropics; Japan's seizure of the South Sea areas handicapped the United Nations. But the USSR was already making most of its own rubber, partly synthetically from chemicals and partly from plantations of plants that once grew wild in Kazakhstan.

The people who once grew wild were also cultivated and developed. Bookstalls in all the railway stations sold technical books on "Road Building," "Courses for Tractor Drivers," "Technical Minimum for Railway Mechanics," "Artificial Insemination of Cattle," and similar themes. Boys began as homeless, starving youngsters looking for jobs to build the railway. They kept on working and studying, and rose to fill important posts.

Alma Ata grew in ten years from a hill town of 60,000 to a garden city of 260,000 with long avenues shaded by poplars and tiny irrigation streams flowing in the gutters, giving coolness to the air. It boasted its new apartment houses; its parks;

its recreation lake for swimming and boating, made by damming the mountain streams. It boasted still more its 7000 university students in fourteen different faculties, preparing to give technical leadership to Kazakhstan's growing life.

"The greatest wealth of a land is people," they repeated in Alma Ata. "We have good people in Kazakhstan."

Here was Satpeinov, the first Kazakh geologist. Born in a nomad herdsman's family, he discovered the biggest copper deposits in the USSR. Here was Berseyev, a Kazakh farmer who claims the world's record in the growing of millet—of which he has secured five metric tons to the acre.

Alma Ata newspapers are full of the exploits of Kazakh farmers, workers, scientists, artists. One night a new opera opens in the Kazakh National Opera House. It is by a Kazakh composer about the history of the Kazakh people. One summer, 1940, the young folks built five hundred miles of railroad to connect Karaganda coal with the iron of Magnet Mountain; the next year they built a longer railroad to the Emba oil.

In a little more than ten years they built 3000 miles of railroad, beginning with the "Turk-Sib." In ten years the industries grew until nearly 1,000,000 people—one-sixth of the population—were employees of industry. The industrial output today equals in value the farming and cattle output. The Kazakhs have a modern land.

This life leaped at once from the nomad epoch to the airplane. To tame the great plains of Kazakhstan the railroad proved too slow. From Alma Ata airport the planes set forth in all directions, exploring the republic's wealth. After they find the riches, they build roads and railroads to get them.

Before the revolution there was only one newspaper in all this territory, for hardly anyone could read. There were only three secondary schools. Today there are 200 newspapers, 600 secondary schools, 8000 grade schools. The State Opera Theater and The National Theater have branches in thirty-five towns.

The most famous man among the Kazakhs is not a warrior nor a government official but the aged minstrel Djambul. He is nearly a hundred years old and has been singing on the plains of Kazakhstan for eighty years.

Djambul was born in 1846, the son of a herdsman. He was gifted with the talent for improvising songs. From the age of fourteen he sang in the herdsmen's camps for a crust of bread or a night's lodging. As a young man, courting, he sang for a whole day before the "yurt" of his beloved, never repeating himself once. But about 1900 Djambul stopped singing. He grew tired of praising the rich and powerful, as Kazakh minstrels, like those of the Middle Ages, were expected to do. He sang the woes of the poor, so he often went hungry.

"Then I began to stoop like an old eagle; my voice weakened and my eyes grew dim."

The revolution made Djambul young again; he was reborn with the rebirth of his people. He sang the songs of the new world, of the iron horse that conquered the desert, of the gardens that bloomed from the wedding of water with the dry soil of the plains. He sang not only about the Kazakhs but about Chinese people and people of Spain and all people everywhere fighting for freedom, and about the coming friendship of the peoples of the world. His best-known poem is his song about Stalin.

Djambul never learned to read, but there were always people eager to read the newspapers to him. All the people of Kazakhstan invited him to live with them. He chose a cooperative farm eighty miles from Alma Ata. They built him a house and gave him a horse; these are all he needs.

Djambul's songs are translated into many languages of the

Djambul's latest song is being recorded in front of his "yurt"

A school library in Djambul—a town named for the national bard

USSR; he is known throughout the Union. On May 20, 1938, a jubilee was celebrated throughout the USSR—the seventy-fifth anniversary of Djambul's singing.

When Hitler struck at the USSR, all the Kazakh people felt it as a personal blow. In 1916 they had rebelled rather than enter labor battalions in the war of the Russian tsar. But in the second World War two-thirds of the elected members of village governments and forty members of the Supreme Soviet of Kazakhstan—their national congress—went to fight on the distant battle front.

Thousands of Kazakhs won decorations in battle. Kazakhs took part in the famous fight of the twenty-eight men of the Panfilov Division, who stopped fifty German tanks at the gates of Moscow and destroyed them all before they themselves were destroyed. Tens of thousands of other Kazakh heroes defended Moscow, Leningrad, Stalingrad.

Kazakhstan had another task in addition to fighting. It must furnish food for the war. In the period 1941–1943, when that world-famous breadbasket the Ukraine was held by the Nazi enemy, Kazakhstan increased both its grain and its meat deliveries, even though its able-bodied men had gone to war. The women, the old men, and the young folks in their teens composed a letter to Stalin, their commander in chief in the fight. They discussed it in hill villages of the Tien Shan Mountains, in the camps on the dry Akmolinsk steppe, on the shores of the salt Aral Sea. They passed it around until they collected nearly a million signatures, all saying: "The brotherhood of the peoples of our great Soviet country has been cemented by the blood shed on the field of battle. We of the rear, whose sons are dying before the great cities of Russia, pledge that the supply of grain and meat shall not fail."

The strain of war, which in 1916 had beggared the people of

Russian Asia to the point of rebellion, now only stimulated the modernized cattle industry of Kazakhstan. Their herds increased right through the war at the rate of more than a million head per year. Their meat deliveries to the front also increased by about 100 million pounds a year. The war hastened the growth of the grain farms also. Millions of farming families from the Ukraine came east with their tractors and joined with the Kazakhs to plow the great plains. Hundreds of factories were also carried on freight trains and set up again in this eastern land.

Fifty-eight geological expeditions set out from Alma Ata in 1942 to explore still further the Kazakh resources. In 1943 there were seventy-four such expeditions, more than during the rapid progress of peacetime. After two years of war the stock-breeding experts of all the Central Asiatic Soviet nations—the Kirghiz, Kazakhs, Uzbeks, Turkmenians, and Tadjiks—met in Alma Ata in the summer of 1943 in a congress "to plan the future development of animal husbandry of Central Asia on the basis of the century-old experience of all its different peoples."

The people of Kazakhstan knew why they were fighting. Where the vultures once hovered over thirst-stricken, dying camels, today the trains of the Turk-Sib speed. The nameless land was found to be a treasure chest and the once-nameless people are its owners. They will hold it for themselves and their allies against all enemies.

UZBEKISTAN, LAND OF WHITE GOLD

COTTON IS THE "white gold" of Central Asia. It was given that name in the Middle Ages when cotton was more valued in Europe than linen, wool, or even silk. Queen Elizabeth of England had a cotton robe to wear on great occasions. Even two hundred years after Elizabeth cotton was still rare and precious, forming only one-tenth of Europe's textiles.

Desire for this "white gold" was one of the causes of wars of conquest by European powers against the peoples of the sunny lands—Egypt, India, China, Central Asia. For cotton is a child of the sun. It demands plenty of light, warmth, good soil, water, and care. It also demands much human labor. After the European powers possessed the sunny lands of Asia, cotton became cheap. This cheapness is due partly to the cotton gin—an American invention that affected much of modern history—and partly to the wide use of cheap, slavelike labor in most of the world's cotton fields.

The Uzbek Republic is chief cotton grower for the USSR. It produces some two-thirds of all the Soviet cotton crop. It consists of a chain of fertile oases in the very heart of Asia, in the foothills of the great ranges. It is nourished by three great rivers and many smaller streams. With an area of 146,000 square miles and a population of 6,500,000 it takes first place among the Central Asian Republics and is the main irrigated district of the USSR. In size and population it is somewhat smaller than California. Its landscape is much like that of California's inland valleys—an irrigated garden with a background of gray mountains and dry plains. Even the climate is the famous California climate, a short, rather rainy winter and a long summer of hot cloudless days.

This fertile region was one of the earliest farming areas in the history of man. Samarkand is its oldest and most famous city. It lies on the Zeravshan River, whose name means "Sower of Gold." Alexander the Great conquered the city and destroyed it in 329 B.C. Ruins near Samarkand indicate a still more ancient city named Afrosaib, supposed to have been founded about 4000–5000 B.C., of which Samarkand was the continuation.

Caravan routes from China to Persia and India met here before the dawn of history. The "golden road to Samarkand" came from the bazaars of Persia; it got its name from the sun-stricken desert sands. The "great road," the "small road," and the "winding way" were various caravan routes from China. When Marco Polo came this way in the thirteenth century on his famous trip from Venice to China, the civilization and the caravan routes were centuries old.

The earliest known people here, according to Professor Viatkin of Samarkand, were the Tadjiks. They lost their fertile lands to later invaders and were pushed into the high mountain valleys of what is Tadjikistan today. The Arabs came in the great Moslem crusades of the seventh and eighth centuries, bringing the religion which is still the faith of the land. They made their capital at Bokhara, at the lower end of the Zeravshan River where it disappears into the desert. It was known as "high, holy, divinely descended Bokhara." Its theological schools made it the religious center of Central Asia. The proverb said: "Samarkand is a jewel on the face of this earth, but Bokhara is the heart of Islam." Since the city was surrounded by malarial swamps and its drinking water came from stagnant pools full of parasitic worms, it was probably the filthiest and most diseased city in the East.

The Mongols of Genghiz Khan conquered this territory thoroughly, destroying Samarkand in A.D. 1220 so completely that it had no life for a hundred years. It came to life again as the capital of Tamerlane. When Tamerlane conquered a country he brought its poets, artists, and architects to Samarkand and ordered them to create here the "light of the world." His brilliant court attracted ambassadors even from Europe. Samarkand became world famous for magnificent mosques, mausoleums, and gorgeous mosaics, many of which remain today.

The Uzbeks next acquired the country. They were a nomad tribe of the great plains, probably related to the Kazakhs. They took the name Uzbek from one of their leaders. It distinguished them as Moslems, opposed to other tribes of their race that still followed the shamans or witch doctors. The Uzbeks were a strong people and are still the dominant folk of Central Asia. They had little culture of their own; but they adopted the culture of the rich cities, since they were of the same religion.

To increase the abundant cotton harvest of Uzbekistan, Uzbek collective farmers discuss plans for their spring sowing of cotton

Russian armies drove into Central Asia in the sixties of the last century. The Russian tsar wanted to restore his prestige, which had suffered when the British defeated him in the Crimean War of 1854–55. An even stronger motive was the need of cotton. Cotton shipments from America to Russia had been stopped by the American Civil War. Hundreds of textile mills in Russia were forced to close. Russian businessmen wanted the cotton of Central Asia. In 1865 the Russian armies took Tashkent, the largest city of Central Asia. Within five years they held all the farms and cities of the cotton regions. It was known as Russian Turkestan. Tashkent was its capital.

A new Russian city of Tashkent grew up beside the native city. It had wide tree-lined boulevards fit for conquerors. A governor's mansion of white marble and a Russian cathedral faced each other across a military parade ground. Scattered Russian settlers came by a new railroad, bringing their own doctors and schools. These schools and doctors were not for the natives, except for a handful who learned Russian and became interpreters and a few native rulers who hired Russian doctors. Natives in their national costumes were not allowed in the streets of the new city of Tashkent.

The land produced wealth, but its people grew poorer. Their soil wore out under the wasteful methods that the new landlords' demand for perpetual cotton crops induced. Central Asia no longer raised its own bread. Its land was all needed for cotton; its bread came from Russia. During the first World War the bread stopped coming. Famine smote Turkestan in 1916. Then the able-bodied men were drafted for "forced labor" in other parts of the Russian Empire, where they died by thousands of cold, hunger, and disease. A great revolt swept Turkestan, spreading to all the native peoples. It was suppressed by Russian divisions brought from the German front. Hundreds of thousands of native people fled over the frontiers into Afghanistan and China, returning only after the Russian Revolution in the years of Soviet rule.

Tashkent, the chief industrial city, became the center of the revolutionary struggle in November, 1917. Russian and native workers joined together—from the railway shops, the cotton gins, the wine presses, the oil presses, and the power plants—against the tsar's corrupt bureaucracy and the native vassal rulers. The conflict was prolonged by the great distance from Moscow and by the intervention of British sepoy troops from India. Soviet government was set up finally and firmly in Tashkent in 1920. For a few years the whole province of Russian Turkestan was governed from Tashkent. In 1924 Soviet Central Asia was divided into separate republics according to nationality.

There are four of these republics in Soviet Central Asia: the Uzbek, the Turkmenian, the Kirghiz, and the Tadjik. The Uzbek Republic is by far the most populous. Holding the central zone of foothills and oases with the great cities—Tashkent, Samarkand, Bokhara—and the cities of the Fergana valley, it has more irrigated land, more people, and more cotton than all the other three republics together. West of it lies Turkmenia in the great deserts; east of it rise the mountain pastures of the Kirghiz and the high valleys of the Tadjiks. North of all these republics stretch the vast plains of Kazakhstan, reaching to faraway Siberia. South of all of Soviet Central Asia lie the frontiers of Afghanistan and Iran.

From Moscow a rather slow train known as the Tashkent Express goes southeast, taking nearly five days to reach the city for which it is named. After a day or so the green farms and forests of central Russia change to dry brown plains and gray desert. The train passes the old fortress town of Orenburg at the southern tip of the Urals, now known as Chkalov after the famous aviator who flew over the North Pole to America. Then the plains grow even browner and the desert sandier as we travel for two days through Kazakhstan. On the fifth morning out of Moscow we wake up in a bright green country with many muddy streams and canals.

Fields are flourishing with bumper crops of alfalfa and cotton. Poplar and mulberry trees shade the long hot roads. Vineyards and orchards cluster around the white flat-roofed houses of villages. Mountains of cotton are heaped at the railway stations. Everywhere we see the oddest type of cart—one whose light body is borne high on two very tall thin wheels. It is well suited to the heavy mud of the irrigated country. It rolls steadily along, with the driver sitting astride the horse.

Even the people in the train show the approach of Asia. Half of them are yellow-skinned, some wearing western clothes but more wearing native costumes of heavy silk. An Uzbek who had the lower berth opposite mine removed his long silk coat five times every day, folded it, placed it on the seat, knelt on top of it, and prayed toward Mecca. It was not always easy to know the right direction from the moving train, but he explained that his religion made allowances for travelers. We were entering the lands of Central Asia, where a common Moslem faith unites many different tribes and nations—nomad shepherds, settled farmers, and city dwellers.

Baskets of roses, asters, chrysanthemums, are on display at all the street corners in the European section of Tashkent. There are booths hung with purple and golden grapes in giant clusters and also selling many kinds of nuts and nut candy. The merchants are swarthy men in turbans or bright plush caps; their loose white clothing exposes their sun-burned chests. Women dress in bright-colored silk, chiefly yellow and red, in a pattern in which the colors shoot into each other in long rays.

The Great Ferghana Canal made this fresh reserve of water possible

Delicious pilafs were prepared for the builders of the canal

Beyond the wide boulevards is the "old town," where the streets are narrow between yellowish clay walls without windows. On the hard-beaten banks of the river are "tea gardens," where men squat on little mats and sip tea slowly and lovingly from flattish cups without handles. Dreamy musicians entertain them by thrumming monotonously on ancient stringed instruments. A grateful breath of coolness rises from the flowing water. The "old town" is no longer sharply separate from the "new town" but is still distinct.

In the old homes of the Uzbeks no windows faced the street. The yellow-gray clay walls opened inward toward a court. Rich people had gardens and a pool in their court. Poor people had only a room or two facing another wall. Women stayed indoors awaiting the pleasure of their lord. If they had to go on the street they covered themselves with long white draperies, with a black horsehair panel over their faces through which they could hardly see. They became hideous walking pillars. Many eye diseases and lung troubles came from wearing this paranja, or veil.

A girl was sold in marriage at the age of nine or ten. She became the property of her husband's parents. She stood behind the husband while he ate; she took his leavings. She was not allowed to talk to her husband or parents-in-law except to answer questions and to whisper: "I obey." Only after the bearing of many sons did a woman become important enough to talk to her elders. The Moslem religion demanded such a life from women, but nomad peoples were not always very strict about it. Uzbeks, being settled folk, were exceptionally severe.

Uzbek homes were well adapted to the climate. They had no chairs and almost no furniture, for lumber was scarce. Uzbeks covered their clay floors with beautiful hand-woven rugs, handed down from generation to generation. In poorer homes these were very dilapidated. Every home had also piles of soft quilts. When people came indoors they took off their dusty shoes at the entrance and sat on quilts on the floor. Bits of china and other family treasures were kept in gaily painted niches cut in the clay wall.

The heat came from a clay oven under the floor. To avoid bringing dirt into the house the fire was fed from outside with straw or cakes of dried dung. The heat rose gently through a small hole, but it was not allowed to escape directly into the room. This would have been very extravagant. Uzbeks did not try to heat the whole room. They put a low round table over the hole and covered it with a heavy quilt which dropped on all sides to the floor. Then people sat around the table and put their slippered or stockinged feet into the grateful warmth below. If they felt very cold they drew the quilt around them, warming themselves to the waist. They offered their guests steaming cups of tea, with fresh or candied fruits from a great brass tray on the table. Doctors claim that this "Uzbek oven" induces chilblains and rheumatism, but some Uzbeks still like the ovens because they are inexpensive and sociable.

The new Soviet law made all the veiled Uzbek women equal with men. Energetic Russian women doctors came to Central Asia to open clinics for Uzbek mothers and babies. They urged the Uzbek women to assert their equality, to throw off their veils and learn to read and write. Most of the Uzbek women were afraid to do this, lest they be murdered by their husbands and by the mullahs—the Moslem priests. No Uzbek court would convict a man for murder if he killed a wife who "dishonored" her family and religion. By 1924 there were just ten unveiled women in the whole Uzbek nation. They had to be guarded day and night against murder.

The "great unveiling" took place on March 7, 1928, in the evening. Preparations were made for more than a year. Uzbeks in government offices were urged: "Be modern; let your wife unveil." In village and city assemblies and in all mothers' clinics this was continuously preached. Everyone knew that a great change was scheduled for March 7, which is International Women's Day.

All the halls in Uzbekistan were reserved that evening for meetings of women only. Russian and native women made speeches, the largest meetings with the most important speakers being in Bokhara—the "heart of Islam." Under the urging of speakers the women tore off their veils and threw them on the platform. They made great processions through the streets, lighted by torches and by bonfires of burning veils.

Progress was slower in the rural districts. Long after unveiled girls were going to school in the cities, the girl students who went to the villages to preach women's rights might be tortured or burned to death. When the Uzbek Dramatic Theater came to Moscow for the All-Union Olympiad in 1930 its performances were framed in two red columns, one of which was half draped in black. The announcer explained that this theater, less than a year old, had already lost three of its performers by murder.

In the past ten years the Central Asian Republic rapidly entered the ranks of modern nations. Part of this was due to the energy released by the new equality of women and the equality of races. The greatest single change was made by the system of cooperative farming, which from 1932 onward gave all farmers equal use of irrigation water and new machines. Uzbek fields are plowed today by 23,000 tractors, replacing the wooden stick-plows that went back to Old Testament days. Their farms show more modern machinery than do the fields of Europe; their airplane lines compare in freight load with western Europe.

The test is in the cotton crop. In the best tsarist years Russia got half a billion pounds of cotton from Central Asia. By 1938 the cotton crop reached three billion pounds and it is still going up. Uzbekistan is chiefly responsible for this increase, for two-thirds of the crop comes from Uzbek fields. Through better farming the average income of Uzbek farm households increased tenfold in the past ten years. Schools are everywhere now; there is compulsory education.

Tashkent is the chief industrial city. It has a population of 600,000. It manufactures millions of yards of cotton fabrics; it also makes farm machinery and fertilizer for the cotton fields. Just outside Tashkent is the seed-selection station of the cotton growers; it claims to be the best equipped in the world. As far back as 1928 it was experimenting with 1500 varieties of cotton from every cotton-growing land on earth. Its experiments have developed varieties that enable the USSR to grow cotton much farther north than it is grown in any other land.

Tashkent is also the most important center of learning in Central Asia. The first university in Central Asia was opened here in 1920. Today the Uzbeks have some thirty institutions of higher learning, most of which are in Tashkent. They have 168 newspapers with a circulation of 1,000,000. One-fifth of the Uzbek population is attending some kind of school.

Tashkent is also an air-traffic center. Many airplanes arrive and leave every day.

Numerous irrigation works have been built in the past decade. The most spectacular construction was that of the great Fergana Canal, built in the summer of 1939 by a great popular movement which set the precedent for canals in Central Asia.

Three thousand farming villages sent word to Stalin that

Nearly every Uzbek man, woman and child wears these embroidered caps called "tiubeteikas"

they needed a canal, not only to produce more cotton but to give pure water to hundreds of villages which for centuries had had only stagnant water to drink. They declared that they would supply all labor if the government would provide materials, machines, and engineers. The proposal was accepted; 200,000 farmers at once volunteered for the work.

On a July morning the villagers of the Fergana valley were awakened by brass trumpets. The farmers took their spades, mattocks, sleeping mats, and hurried to the village market place to be assigned to work. On foot, in carts, and by auto trucks they moved from all over Fergana to the construction site like an army going into battle. The front—in other words, the digging work—was 162 miles long. Camps sprang up; farm women came to cook meals; even the boys and girls from twelve to fourteen years old acted as postmen between the camps. Eighteen hundred of the best singers and dancers of Uzbekistan came to perform for the campers after the day's work.

Twenty-three million cubic yards of earth had to be excavated. Normally such a canal would take several years to dig. One hundred and sixty thousand farmers of the Fergana valley dug it in forty-five days and got home for the cotton picking in September. The digging of this canal thrilled all Central Asia. Seventy smaller canals soon followed it, built in the same way —the government furnishing engineers, materials, and machinery, while the farmers who wanted the water did the work.

When Hitler's armies invaded the USSR, the lands of Central Asia were asked to take in millions of refugees. People without homes, often without proper clothing, could survive in this warm climate better than in colder northern lands. Three million refugees were sheltered by the Uzbeks, a number equal

An outdoor lunch in Uzbekistan consisting of tea, flat cakes, fruits and other Uzbek foods

to half their previous population. Tens of thousands of war orphans were permanently adopted. One Uzbek farmer started an "international family" by adopting five orphans, each of a different nationality but all of them citizens and war victims of the USSR.

Those once-closed homes where women were imprisoned took in outsiders with the slogan "No Uzbek family without an evacuated child."

Three million more mouths to feed and no grain could come from Russia! The Uzbek farmers, with the help of the refugees, plowed 2,000,000 acres of virgin land for wheat, without interfering with their cotton. They kept on building irrigation works. The North Tashkent Canal, built during the war, reclaimed more than 2,000,000 acres. Sugar beets were planted there to replace sugar lost by the seizure and devastation of the Ukraine. Beginning with 1942, the Uzbeks planted two crops a year in their wheat fields. They harvested the winter wheat in June and then planted millet and other fast-ripening crops.

During the war Uzbekistan became a land of mighty industry. The people claim that their industries were increased sixfold by the factories that moved here from the regions seized by Hitler. The output of electric power in January, 1943, was 50 per cent higher than before the war. Many new hydroelectric stations were being built. The first big steel works in Central Asia opened in 1944.

Scientific work also continued. In August, 1943, in the midst of war, there appeared the first two volumes of the *History of the Peoples of Uzbekistan*. It was compiled by the Uzbek branch of the Academy of Sciences. It announced itself proudly but accurately as the "first systematic history of the peoples who more than once have influenced not only Central Asia but the history of the world."

TURKMENIANS, THE PEOPLE OF THE SANDS

"WATER, NOT EARTH, GIVES LIFE" is the saying of the Turkmenians. Water is the hero of most of their legends. Water created and destroyed their farms and cities, changed farmers into migratory herdsmen, drove the people into tribal conflicts and wars. Their story for a thousand years is the story of the fight for water. The Turkmenians live where our planet is slowly drying. They are the people of the desert sands.

Turkmenia lies due east of the Caspian Sea and due north of Iran and Afghanistan. Its 171,250 square miles of area make it half again as large as Arizona, while, with its population of 1,300,000, it is about twice as thickly settled as that state. More than four-fifths of the territory—all the center and northern

part—is filled by the Kara-kum desert. The name means "black
sands." It is one of the most lifeless deserts in the world and is
large enough to enclose all the British Isles.

Most of the people of Turkmenia live along the southern
edge of the country in the foothills of the range that forms
their frontier with Iran. Here the mountain streams create a
fringe of vegetation and of human life. Here lies ancient Ashkhabad, the Turkmenian capital. Here the railroad runs from
the Caspian Sea eastward to Uzbekistan. Another fringe of life
lies along the eastern border of Turkmenia where the great
Amu River nourishes a chain of oases. There are a few fishing
ports on the Caspian, but they find it difficult to get fresh water
or any vegetable food. The shores of the Caspian Sea are either
gleaming white cliffs or salt marshes that were once great bays.
The drying of the Caspian has left a flat clay desert for hundreds of miles eastward, with only an occasional water well.

On most of the maps of Turkmenia you see neither rivers nor
cities but only the names of wells. People live even in the sands
of the Kara-kum. No desert in the world is entirely made of
sand. If you fly over the desert in springtime you will see that
there is quite a bit of green. For part of the year there is grass on
which camels and sheep can feed. A migratory life of cameltenders and sheepherders has existed for centuries around the
water that lies deep underground in wells. Thousands of years
of experience have taught people how to find water in the most
unexpected places.

Strange forms of life exist in the desert. There are rubber-
bearing bushes and plants that are valuable for medicine. There
are lizards six feet long that remind us of the prehistoric beasts
before human beings were on earth. The koulan, a kind of wild
ass, is able to endure great hardship. There is a desert gazelle
that lives for months without water, getting its moisture from
vegetation.

As our earth grows drier the "black sands" swallow everything. Rivers rise in the southern mountains and flow northward but finally vanish in sand. Even the mighty Amu, too large to be entirely swallowed, has been steadily retreating. In ancient times it boldly crossed the desert and entered the Caspian. With the passing of centuries the sand and silt carried by the river raised its mouth, turning the river backward into the Aral Sea. Thus the great Amu has been slowly committing suicide.

Great cities have been swallowed by the Kara-kum. According to an ancient Turkmenian manuscript, Kunia-Urgench was a lively town in the thirteenth century. It was surrounded by aspen groves and claimed the "tallest minaret in the world." There is neither city nor aspen grove today but only the minaret sticking up through the sand. In the sixteenth century an English merchant named Johnson traveled the caravan route to Khiva along the northern edge of what is today Turkmenia. He reported many busy towns and villages, but today the sand has covered them all.

The vanishing of all this human life was not caused by the desert alone. Centuries of wars exhausted the people. Most of these wars were for water.

In peaceful times each tribe had its canal and regulated the control of water. There were conflicts even inside the tribe, for water control was the road to wealth and power. Water for irrigation was part of the dowry of brides; it was denied to bachelors, childless people, widows, orphans, and the insane. Water was measured by time. An ordinary family might have "fifteen minutes of water once in twelve days." Some poor men got only "three minutes," and since this was useless they were forced to sell their water to some richer man and to work for him in his fields. As a tribe grew, more water was needed and the struggle for it grew sharper. This led to wars between tribes.

Water was not only a reason for war but also a weapon. Rulers subdued unruly tribes by shutting off their water. The Emir of Bokhara conquered the people of Merv in the eighteenth century by smashing their dam so that their water and their food supply dried up. What the conquerors began the desert finished. The "black sands" covered canals, gardens, and streets. People who had once been farmers on irrigated land were forced to become herdsmen on patches of grass in the desert. Eve this did not stop the fight over water. When irrigation streams were gone the people still fought for the wells.

Centuries ago the Russians knew that people lived in the "black sands." Black-bearded men in bright-colored robes and enormous fuzzy sheepskin caps came to the Russian market in Orenburg. They brought sheepskins, leather, silk, opium, and beautiful deep-red rugs that went into the world markets and became famous. When these men left Orenburg, it took them several months by camel to get home.

Peter the Great sent an expedition of 7000 men into the Kara-kum in 1715 to find out what had happened to the great Amu River that once entered the Caspian Sea. It was rumored that the Uzbeks in fighting the Turkmenians had turned the river by a dam in order to starve the people of the sands. Peter intended to smash that dam and bring the river back to the Caspian. Thus he would have a waterway from the heart of Russia almost to India by the Volga River, the Caspian, and the Amu. The expedition never reported about the dam; none of the seven thousand came back.

The British government also took an interest in Turkmenia. They knew that it lay on the road from Russia to India. British travelers and government agents visited it and described it in travel books—among them Lieutenant Burns of the East India

Turkmenian karakul from lambs like these is known the world over

Their carpets are equally famous—the industry employs 24,000 women

Company, who explored it in 1831. For nearly a century the "black sands" of the Turkmenians formed a kind of no man's land between two rival empires, the Russians expanding on the north and the British on the south.

In 1873 the Russian general Skobelev was sent to "absorb" the territory. His ship set forth from Baku on the western shore of the Caspian and landed on the great desert of the eastern shore. The soldiers began to lay a railroad eastward, fighting the Turkmenians as they went. General Skobelev paid hunters three rubles a head for killing Turkmenians. They proved it by bringing back the heads or the ears. "These people are a black spot on the earth," wrote the general. "Their extermination would be a wholly virtuous act."

The Turkmenians were equally ruthless. They went to the wells ahead of the Russians and threw dead dogs into them. They knew the laws of the sands: to poison the wells was to close the desert. The Russians had little understanding of the desert. One general ordered a forced march straight across the sands to Khiva. They started with thousands of barrels of water, but this rapidly evaporated in the terrible heat. Men went insane from the endless mirages. Only a handful reached the well of Ort, which was considered halfway. None of them got to Khiva.

The Turkmenians had secret help from Great Britain; Great Britain, however, was not sufficiently interested in Turkmenia to fight the Russians for it directly. The Turkmenians fought stubbornly but lacked modern weapons. They had not even a united government; they were scattered, disunited tribes.

So, in spite of reckless losses of Russian soldiers, the Russian railroad moved onward into the desert. Its rails were often covered by the blowing sands. Its path was whitened by the bones of Turkmenians and Russians. But the tsar succeeded in building the railroad and in using it to hold the Turkmenians down. The irrigated lands were taken by Russian officers. The best oasis, Murgabak, became a tsar's estate.

The Turkmenians retreated into the mountains and the deserts. Tribal wars for water increased, decimating the tribesmen. There seemed no escape from thirst and hunger and bondage. The Turkmenians, hardened for centuries against the desert, began to die out under the Russian tsar.

The railroad, once built for the tsar's conquest, carried the revolution to the Turkmenians in 1917. Railway workers became the leaders; every railway town was a citadel of revolt. British sepoy troops from India, thinking Turkmenia unguarded, came in from Persia in August, 1918. The railway workers preached revolt to these Indian troops as well as to the Turkmenians. Eventually the British withdrew. Soviet rule was established in Central Asia.

The Republic of Turkmenia was set up in 1924 when the province known as Russian Turkestan was divided into its separate nationalities. The Turkmenians knew little of government and the Russians who helped them knew little of the desert. In 1925 an expedition from the Moscow Academy of Sciences, which went to the Kara-kum to prospect for minerals, discovered 100,000 "people of the sands" who had never heard of any Soviet government, either the one in Moscow or the one in Ashkhabad, which had "ruled" them for a year.

These people lived widely scattered around some 2000 wells. They had no doctors. Not one man in a hundred could read. They had 3,000,000 head of cattle—camels, sheep, and goats. The cattle and the wells belonged to the rich men, whom the poorer men served as herdsmen.

Committees of local herdsmen were at once formed to take possession of the wells as the property of all the people. Doctors, teachers, women's organizers, and buyers of wool came into this formerly unknown region. Finally big cooperative cattle and sheep ranches were organized, using the pastures by rational plan.

Soviet scientists made a long-range plan for the conquest of the desert.

An individual herdsman cannot conquer the desert. He can make a well, but he cannot bind the sands. He may trace the footprints of a vanished river, but he cannot bring its waters back. Even a tribe or a dozen tribes cannot conquer the desert. They fight for water and handle it wastefully. They cut down the scanty plants for food and fuel and make the land bare. But when the water of Turkmenia became the property of the whole people, the scientists decided that man could conquer the desert. They challenged even the drying of the planet in the retreat of its Glacial Age.

First they improved irrigation. The canal builders followed the water courses from the mountains downward, planning the best use of every stream. Old canals were improved and new canals were dug. Some streams went underground at the foot of the mountains; work began to bring these to the surface. The greatest plan is to turn the Amu River back to its ancient channel. This is a long-range project which will take many years. It will bring fresh water to the eastern shore of the Caspian, which now imports water on steamers from the other side of the sea. It will create large areas of irrigated farming in the old bed of the river, whose silt is more fertile than that of the Nile.

Canals can reach only a small part of the great Kara-kum. A scientific station for "sand research" was set up at Repetek in the desert. Seed was brought from Morocco, from Tripoli, and from the deserts of the United States. Two hundred varieties of cattle feed were sown in 1933 to try to find a stable winter feed. Two hundred kinds were sown and 195 perished. Five survived.

The scientists learned many things about the sand. They learned that the winter snow sank underground and made a reserve of moisture that could be tapped by wells. It could also be reached by plants with very deep roots. A deep-rooted grass already grew in parts of the Kara-kum, providing pasture for sheep. If too many sheep grazed on this grass they broke up the pasture and it blew away into sand dunes.

Airplanes began to fly over the desert every winter under the direction of the scientists. They sow "sand oats" and similar plants on the thin snow. The plants take root as the snow melts. They develop long roots that follow the moisture far down into the sand. They "bind the sands" so that they become a stable pasture instead of blowing about into sand dunes. The Turkmenian government, under direction of the scientists, regulates all sheep and cattle grazing so that pastures will not be broken up.

The Repetek scientists were not content with making pastures in the desert. They wanted to make grain farms, vegetable gardens, vineyards, and fruit orchards in the very center of the sands where there were no rivers or irrigation canals. They developed three varieties of wheat that would grow where the rainfall is only 1.9 inches a year. This is five times as dry as Nevada, the driest state in America, with an average rainfall of 9.22 inches.

To grow vegetables the scientists dug trenches fifteen feet deep to reach the underground moisture, and with sloping sides to admit just enough sun. The harsh desert climate is actually moderated in these trenches. They protect the plants from the dry winds that parch them by day and freeze them by night. Good soil was put in the bottom of the trenches. Here many kinds of vegetables are successfully grown—carrots, beets, cabbage, cucumbers, lettuce, tomatoes—and many kinds of grapes, berries, and fruits. Even flowers are grown, including twenty varieties of roses. Apple trees are grown, protected by lines of poplars.

Scientists say they have only begun the conquest of the desert. But the driest, hottest parts of the "black sands" already produce grain, vegetables, fruit, and flowers.

Desert farms are not expected to compete in farming with the easily watered parts of the USSR. Their purpose is to provide fresh food for people who seek the desert's riches in other ways.

Rich sulphur deposits were long known to exist in the "black sands." They were not developed, for they were too hard to reach. The new Turkmenian government decided that such riches should be used. They opened an airplane line to the sulphur for passengers and high-class freight. They brought the sulphur out by camels. Then they invented wide auto tires that could cross the sand. Finally they built roads. Truck caravans of sulphur replaced the camel caravans. Trench farms supply fresh food to the sulphur-mining settlements.

Unusual chemical riches are found on a great gulf of the Caspian where shallow water evaporates very rapidly, leaving valuable salts. These salts have accumulated into great ridges that are easily worked. Nobody could live here formerly. Now there is a chemical plant and a town. Most of the chemical workers are former cameltenders. Fresh food comes from trench farms.

So many new industries were built on the minerals of Turkmenia that by 1939 the industrial output was far ahead of the farm and cattle output, forming 70 per cent of all wealth produced. A use was found for even the sand of the desert. A great glass factory uses it to make 40,000,000 square feet of high-quality glass a year.

Turkmenian horses are some of the world's strongest

Barley from irrigated lands   *Sulphate fields on the Caspian*

Cotton was always grown in the Turkmenian oases. Today the fringe of farm life on the southern and eastern edges of the country is extended through improved irrigation so that the cotton area is two and a half times what it was in tsarist days. Its yield has doubled through wide use of machinery and better farm methods. Sheep breeding comes next to cotton. Turkmenian karakul—made from the soft skin of unborn lambs—is famous all over the world.

Turkmen take great pride in their horses. Outside experts formerly held that these animals were useful only for short rides under desert conditions. Turkmenians disagreed. They decided to show off their horses to all the people in the USSR and to prove them the best horses in the world.

A fifty-five-year-old horseman named Kabysh-Mamysh led a horseback trip all the way to Moscow. The horsemen started from Ashkhabad toward the end of May in 1935, crossed the "black sands" in the heat of June, rode through the desolate Ust-Urda steppe and through all the farmlands of southeastern Russia. They reached Moscow in mid-August, having traveled 2580 miles in less than three months.

A tremendous guard of honor met them on the highway far out of Moscow; thousands of bicyclers, horsemen, and pedestrians escorted them to town. They were given a celebration at the Hippodrome. Stalin congratulated them on their "glorious victory." The Turkmenian horses were used thereafter for cross-breeding in the Red Army cavalry. They had been proved one of the strongest strains in the world.

Turkmenia, once thirst-stricken and hungry, is now beginning to prosper. It is a land where the air mail connects with the camel post. A hundred miles beyond the railway the planes toss their mailbags to waiting caravans. Turkmenians send letters now, and more than half of them have learned to read and write. The rest are learning rapidly. Even the girls go to school. Before the revolution there were only two girls in school in all Turkmenia.

A Turkmenian branch of the Academy of Sciences was opened in 1941, with 50 research institutions employing 500 scientific workers. Its first task is to explore and develop Turkmenia. Turkmenia has also 60 newspapers, several publishing houses, and a national theater. It has 4 institutions of higher learning and 30 technical schools.

The second World War raised special problems for Turkmenia. It was one of the countries to which many enterprises were evacuated from the occupied parts of the USSR. These new workers had to be fed. Grainlands in 1942 increased 60 per cent over the previous year. A fuel problem arose when the oil was needed for the Red Army; Turkmenia met it by developing local deposits of coal. As a special gift to the Red Army the Turkmenians sent fur-lined coats, felt boots, quilted jackets of their cotton, mittens knit from their wool.

Turkmenians were always brave in defense of their country. Once they fought for their land against the Russians. Now they defend their land by defending Russia too. They sent their sons to the front with the other peoples of the Soviet Union. Thus these men of the sands became part of the great struggle of the United Nations for a better, freer world.

KIRGHIZ, HERDSMEN OF THE HIGH PASTURES

THE KIRGHIZ are the people of the high pastures. In the far southeast corner of the USSR, where the great mountain ranges of India, China, and the Soviet Union run together, they tend their cattle and sheep on the "roof of the world."

Kirghizia is larger than all of New England but somewhat smaller than Idaho; it has 75,926 square miles. Nearly all of it is mountain pasture; there are 28,000,000 acres of pasture and 2,500,000 acres of cultivated soil. This gives every Kirghiz man, woman, and baby—there are 1,500,000 of them—an acre and two-thirds of farmland to cultivate and twenty acres of pastureland in which to roam.

KIRGHIZ

Wild rivers run down from the pastures of the Kirghiz. They run west to the cotton lands of the Uzbeks, north to the Kazakh plains, east to the rice fields of Chinese Turkestan. Kirghizia gives the water of life to all her neighbors. Most of the great rivers of Central Asia are born in her glaciers and hills. The Kirghiz live above the dry plains of the Kazakhs, above the irrigated valleys of the Uzbeks. They live above and beyond all other peoples.

Not always were the Kirghiz confined to these high pastures. Old Chinese manuscripts tell of a Kirghiz Empire before the Christian era; they called it Chian-chun. It rivaled great China. Its warriors raided Peking. Then for a thousand years the Kirghiz disappeared from history; for they were an illiterate folk, leaving few records.

They were a people on horseback, following where the grass grows. They camped in "yurts," round tents of felted wool. They lived on milk and meat from their herds. In winter they moved downward into the valleys and huddled in settlements under some sheltering cliff. In spring they took up their trek to the heights. All summer they camped in the thick grass of mountain meadows, visiting from camp to camp, celebrating festivals and weddings, lazily sunning themselves as they watched their cattle and sheep.

Thus they lived for twenty centuries while one conqueror after another seized the lowlands, built cities and palaces and temples of famous beauty, and destroyed what other conquerors had built. The Kirghiz built nothing, and kept nothing except their pastures and their love of freedom. Each new conqueror forced them a little farther into the hills and made their life a little harder than before.

The Kirghiz adapted themselves to their pastures. They became good campers. Their "yurts" are far superior to a modern

205

tent. They became good caravan men, traveling across all the boundaries that meet on the "roof of the world." They became milk specialists, making a variety of milk products not only from cows' milk but from the milk of ewes and mares and yaks, odd-looking mountain animals that the Kirghiz tamed. But they had no book learning; they had not even an alphabet. By songs that passed from singer to singer they kept their unity as a people, holding the high pastures for two thousand years.

The life of a nomad herdsman is not romantic. It is full of hardship and loss. When an unexpected blizzard spread a coating of ice on the pastures, entire herds perished. In some winters the Kirghiz thus lost half their cattle. When herds from many valleys met for the lazy summers they often brought diseases, and pestilence swept the herds. The Kirghiz had no doctors or veterinaries. They had only sorcerers who "cured" by magic charms.

The grass of the Kirghiz is important in world history. It created the great hoards of wealth that the princes of India have today. A three-cornered trade went on for centuries between India, China, and Russia. The exports from western China are furs and sheepskins, which are too heavy to send over the grassless Himalayan passes. These heavy goods went to Russia and Europe because the caravan animals could eat Kirghiz grass all the way. The Chinese took their pay in gold and silver from Europe and sent them to India to buy fine silks and luxury goods that they desired. The latter were light and valuable and it paid to bring them even over the high grassless pass of the Karakorum from India to Chinese Turkestan. Thus the riches of Europe were heaped up in India because of the Kirghiz grass.

The Kirghiz held out longer against the Russian conquerors than did any other people of Central Asia.

Their last stand was led in 1875 by a famous woman known as the "empress of the Alai pastures," a chieftain's widow who

All members of Kirghiz families prepare for the trip to summer pastures in the Alai; "koumiss" is served to guests in a bag of skin

ruled through her sons. The Russians captured her on her trek to winter quarters and induced her to sign a "treaty of alliance." She had a tragic fate. Her eldest son disowned her and fled to Mecca. Two of her younger sons quarreled with a Russian official and slew him. They were executed and the empress-mother went insane from grief. When I visited Kirghizia in 1929 the grandson of the "empress" still lived there and was much revered by the older folk.

Russian settlers pushed higher and higher into the valleys, taking the best of the Kirghiz lands. The Kirghiz, who had survived all other conquerors, began to die out under the rule of the Russian tsar. In the ten years before the first World War their population decreased by 10 per cent. Their greatest tragedy came in 1916 as a result of the war. The tsar's army needed more meat than Russian civilians had ever dreamed of eating. They took the cattle and sheep from the Kirghiz, paying in paper rubles that were useless to the shepherd folk. The animals were wastefully slaughtered; there was no cold storage in Central Asia. The beggared Kirghiz, moving sadly along the mountain trails, saw tens of thousands of their dead sheep rotting. Then came the decree that the "native peoples" must be drafted for labor under an alien sun.

"Where is this war to which we must go?" asked the Kirghiz.

"A whole year's journey by three fast horses," was the reply.

The Kirghiz revolted blindly. Their revolt spread to all of the native peoples. From the blue Caspian Sea to the borders of China the native folk killed Russians. The Russian army put them down, slaying tens of thousands of Kirghiz. The terrified Kirghiz fled over the border into China as winter was coming on. Old men, women, and babies froze to death in the snow. Others reached the oases of Chinese Turkestan on foot and starving and sold their children into slavery that some might keep alive.

"We fled in 1916 and returned in 1918," said the superintendent of schools of Kirghizia to me years later. "We lost nearly a third of our people and more than two-thirds of our cattle. Did any other nation lose as much in the first World War?"

The new Soviet government sent expeditions to the Kirghiz. They sent doctors, teachers, organizers, caravans for trade. They told the Kirghiz that the pastures and the valleys of Kirghizia belonged to the Kirghiz people and that Russians would come only to teach them modern ways. They told them to chose their own government and to elect representatives to the federal government in Moscow.

It took some time for the Kirghiz to grasp these ideas. The first trading expedition disappeared without a trace. The Kirghiz took the iron pots, cotton goods, tea and sugar, and the man in charge never got back. A woman doctor who went on the first health expedition told me that the Kirghiz crowded around her in great excitement, showing their diseases and asking for help. Then they demanded: "Tell us the word that you use so that we may use it when you are gone." Medicine to them was a kind of magic. When she said that there was no magic word they grew angry.

By 1929 when I first visited Kirghizia the new policy had begun to work. Russians and Kirghiz worked together in the district governments. The president of southern Kirghizia, for instance, was a Kirghiz who had learned to read and write since the revolution. Other newly educated Kirghiz held most of the government posts. There was a Russian vice-president who acted as interpreter to outsiders, and Russians were in charge of finance and health because the Kirghiz had not had time to learn banking or medicine. They were learning fast, for every Kirghiz boy knew that as soon as he gained education he would replace some Russian in a government post.

Thirty bandits were on trial in the city of Osh, an ancient trading post whose traditions go back to Alexander the Great. They had been looting the farms of those Kirghiz who were trying to settle on the soil. The farmers had formed a vigilance committee, rounded up and almost lynched the bandits. The police saved the offenders for trial.

Court was held in a large room jammed with Kirghiz witnesses and onlookers. The judge was Russian, but the two "co-judges"—selected from the people, decision being by unanimous agreement of all three—were Kirghiz, one a coal miner, the other a woman textile worker with a red kerchief on her black hair. The bandit ringleaders were condemned to death, for they had killed many people. The lesser bandits got jail sentences, which were applauded by the crowd.

"This is the first time that the Kirghiz community has supported civilized law against other Kirghiz," a Russian onlooker said.

A new experiment in government was being tried that year in the high pastures. It was hard to carry the new ideas to the winter settlements, separated by snowy ranges; but it was easy to reach all the Kirghiz in summer, when they met in the open grass. A special traveling government was therefore sent to the Vale of Alai, the principal southern pasture, sixty miles long by twenty wide at 10,000 feet elevation. To visit this "soviet of the high pastures" we set out on the Kirghiz trail.

For many days we rode through steep green hills sprinkled with red and yellow poppies, by muddy boiling streams that cut through high cliffs. Hundreds of Kirghiz were traveling in family groups to the pastures. Whenever I chose to walk on the trail all Kirghiz stared at me and asked in pity: "Have you lost your horse?" They could not understand anyone walking if it was possible to ride. Kirghiz babies learn to ride before they learn to walk. I have seen a nursing baby less than a year old cry to be put on a horse.

Under the cliffs of the upper valleys were many of the Kirghiz winter settlements. They were deserted; the people had gone higher up for the summer grass. Apparently no attempt had been made to locate near water. The nearest stream was often a mile away. The settlements were only for winter, when the streams are frozen and water is secured by melting snow. The chief need in winter is shelter. The chosen sites were always protected on two or three sides by high cliffs. The structures were placed close to the steepest hillside, where the winds and snowdrifts would be least. Most of the structures were stables for cattle. The people did not live in buildings but in the "yurts," which they brought back from the pastures and for which permanent platforms had been made.

Patches of barley, ragged and full of weeds, grew near many of the stables. The owner neglected this crop until autumn and then pitched it into the stable for winter feed. The Russian expedition with which I traveled spent a hot afternoon measuring barley patches and trying to translate the Kirghiz land measurements into the metric system. The Kirghiz had two measures of land: a "cheksi," apronful, and a "cheikrek," horseload. This meant the amount of land that an apronful or a horseload of barley would sow. This measurement seems vague by modern standards but was adequate to a nomad's needs.

Beyond the deserted winter settlements we came to the summer camps, clusters of a few "yurts" guarded by fierce dogs and surrounded by peaceful cattle and sheep browsing in deep grass. The Kirghiz greeted us hospitably. They were especially pleased by gifts of small hard candies for the children. Sugar has only recently been known among them and is still a great luxury. One old man accepted a chunk of hard sugar, licked it

*These narrators are dictating from memory the 400,000 lines of poetry
which make up the "Manas"—epic ballad of Kirghiz fame*

twice, and passed it to his wife. She also licked it twice and put
it in her bosom, patting it like a cherished baby. The women
asked for soap. For centuries they have cleaned house with fire
and water, but now they are eager for the new convenience of
soap.

In return they offered us milk in many forms. The commonest form was "airann," sour milk boiled to the consistency of
thin porridge. It is the Kirghiz staple food. When they learned
that I preferred sweet milk they gave it to me but looked at me
as if they deplored my taste. The men offered "koumiss," a
mildly intoxicating beverage made of mare's milk and considered the drink of honor. There were many forms of curd
similar to cheese, and a heavy white fat stuff known as "keimak"
—a kind of substitute for butter and cream.

KIRGHIZ

The Kirghiz "yurts" were very comfortable for camping. Their thick felt was a much better protection against both the heat of the broiling sun and the chill of the cold mountain nights than was the thin canvas of our tents. The ground inside was usually covered by a carpet of dark-colored felt, ornamented by white patterns. On it were heaped many quilts for comfort in sitting and for warmth at night. A fire built on stones in the center of the "yurt" served both for warmth and for cooking. The smoke escaped more or less directly through a hole in the center of the roof, which also admitted light. An iron pot on a tripod was usually boiling over the fire, this ironware being the chief thing the nomads buy from civilization.

All Kirghiz home comfort is produced by the women. They make the "yurt," rolling the heavy felt and then decorating it. They milk the cattle and ewes and turn the milk into food products that keep for a considerable time in the changing

Kirghiz women join in the harvest campaign of their local collective farm

climate. They make most of the household containers from the intestines of cattle and sheep.

Women were valuable property among the Kirghiz until the new Soviet law set them free. They did such heavy work and bore so many children without medical care that the death rate among them was very high. Therefore girls brought a higher price among the Kirghiz than among any other people in Central Asia.

The Kirghiz women were as curious to know about me as I was to know about them. They especially wanted to know how my husband had given me permission to go so far away from home. When I told them that I had no husband and could travel as I chose, they struggled with the new idea and made the interpreter repeat it several times. So it was really possible for a woman to live without a master! They nodded in excitement. The oldest woman stared at me for a long time and then said emphatically: "Good! Very good!"

A cold hostile look came into the faces of the men. It was the first time I had seen such a look on a Kirghiz face. Many of the native people were at that time killing the "agitators for women's rights." No foreigner had been killed, but I was glad to get out of that "yurt."

The traveling government of the high pastures included a trading post, two or three schools in different parts of the valley, a medical station, a women's organizer, and a district court.

A red flag with the "hammer and sickle" flew over the trading post, which consisted of two "yurts" housing tea, sugar, and brightly colored cotton goods and surrounded by piles of sheepskins and iron pots. Trading was largely by direct barter of city wares for sheepskins and wool. The government trader was a hardy Russian who had learned to squat on the ground like a Kirghiz. By cutting out all middlemen he exchanged goods at lower than city prices. His purpose was to win the friendship of the Kirghiz and to increase their wool production. He also helped the poor Kirghiz against the richer by selling goods to everyone; formerly only those who had many skins to sell could afford to make the long trip to the city, while the poorer had to send their goods through the richer men and take in return whatever they could get.

The district court was held in a "yurt," while culprits and complainants waited their turn on the grass outside. The judge, a Kirghiz in corduroy blouse and fuzzy fur cap, squatted on a rug. Two dark-skinned women with shawls on their heads were the "cojudges" from the local population. The clerk of the court lay flat on his stomach for better ease in writing, placing paper and ink in front of him on the ground.

Despite this informality it was a very serious court. One case was that of a sheepherder suing for payment of wages. He had worked for a year and a half for a richer Kirghiz without a wage agreement. He had received some gifts of food and a few advances in money. His master proposed to pay him off at the rate of twenty rubles a month, at that time about ten dollars. The sheepherder could not read or write, but he had heard of a shepherds' trade union whose wage scale was thirty-six rubles a month. He demanded the union rate and the court supported him.

A case of bride purchase came next. This was a criminal offense. The bride, a sixteen-year-old girl dressed in all the colors of the rainbow, had been sold the previous winter for two horses, thirty sheep, and two hundred rubles. She was brought to court with her young husband and with the fathers of both. The judge gave a hot lecture on the "crime" of selling women and proposed to make an example by sending both the fathers to jail. The two women cojudges felt that jail was too severe. Confinement is terrible to a free-roving Kirghiz. A compromise sentence gave eight months "forced labor" without confinement. The men could stay at home but must do work of public benefit, such as road building.

All around the "Soviet of the High Pastures" were the signs of the old, roving life. I saw a festival in honor of a visiting Kirghiz chieftain. Nearly a hundred guests came on horses gaily decked with silver trappings and red cloth embroidered with heavy fringe. In a large open space they played the national sport known as "baiga." A goat was killed and tossed among the men, who fought for it on horseback in a game resembling polo. The winner threw it proudly at the feet of the guest of honor. Then the older men squatted on the ground to cheer their sons in the horse races, carried on by boys in their teens. The winner was a lad of fifteen.

Kolpaief, superintendent of schools for southern Kirghizia, who was spending his summer in educational work in the high pastures, stated that the Kirghiz had already not only an alphabet and a written language but authors and a national theater. They were writing down the old Kirghiz songs. A scientific committee was introducing into the language the scientific terms for which the Kirghiz had no equivalent, and was writing textbooks on science.

The Kirghiz were slow to start; but when once they had started, their speed made up the handicap of two thousand years. In 1918 the first Soviet government was set up in Kirghizia. In 1926 the Kirghiz Autonomous Republic was formed. In 1936 Kirghizia became a sovereign republic with the right to secede. The year 1939 is a landmark in Kirghiz history; in that year the last of the nomads acquired a settled home. In 1944, barely twenty years after they got an alphabet, the Kirghiz with fifteen other Soviet republics gained the right to have

A Kirghiz woman lands at the airport in Frunze—by parachute

their own army and to send ambassadors to world capitals.

The twenty-one miles of auto road that existed in 1928 grew by 1943 to 2400 miles, more than a hundred times as many. A north-south highway crosses all the high ridges, connecting the mountain pastures with the farms. The mountain streams have been harnessed to 134 electric power plants serving new industries. A million new irrigated acres have been added to the 1,500,000 they formerly possessed. Just before the second World War 30,000 Kirghiz farmers, inspired by the great Fergana Canal of the Uzbeks, turned out to dig the great Chu Canal and removed 9,000,000 cubic yards in forty days.

The Kirghiz people, who were dying out under the tsar, now claim to be increasing faster than any other people in the world. In a little over twelve years, from December, 1926, to

January, 1939, the population increased 45 per cent. These once-nomad herdsmen also claim the world's highest average cotton yield in their irrigated fields. The world average yield outside the USSR is 176 pounds per acre; the American average is 264 pounds per acre; the average in the USSR is 352 pounds per acre, while the Kirghiz average—on some 57,000 irrigated acres—was 1540 pounds per acre in 1938, nine times as high as the world average.

These people, who had no schools in their own language, have now six institutions of higher learning and thirty-six technical schools, besides grade schools in all the villages. They have sixty-seven newspapers, a national picture gallery, a national theater, a philharmonic orchestra, and a motion-picture studio making Kirghiz motion pictures.

The Kirghiz have taken part in the second World War wholeheartedly. Besides sending their men to fight they have sent millions of pounds of meat. They also made a free donation to the Red Army of more than 100,000 sheepskins and large quantities of wool and felt boots. They sent forty-three carloads of concentrated food products to besieged Leningrad.

A Moslem priest of northern Kirghizia gave the reason why he sent his two oldest sons to war: "If the Hitlerite Germans win they trample on human dignity, persecute other races and religions, and bring slavery a hundred times worse than under the tsar. That is why we Kirghiz do everything we can to help the Red Army, which guards our freedom and our human rights."

TADJIKS LIVE ON A STAIRCASE OF MOUNTAINS

A BUDDHIST MONK of the sixth century wrote about the land where the Tadjiks live today: "This is the central point of earth and heaven. Here is the lake in which the dragon dwells."

The Tadjiks live on a kind of giant staircase that does seem to lead from earth to heaven, with mountains for the steps. The hot dry lands below are watered by two swift rivers: the Syr in the north and the Amu, which curves around the country in the south—separating it from Afghanistan. Both rivers are only a few hundred feet above sea level at the place where they leave Tadjikistan. The air quivers in a reddish haze of heat over the sandbanks, while tigers prowl in the wet jungles.

The land starts up steeply from the level of the rivers until it reaches a high, tremendous plateau edged with still higher mountains. These are the Pamirs, known as the "roof of the world." There is a fairly large lake where nothing much could live but the "dragon," for there is practically no vegetation and the climate is eternally uncomfortable. The sun blazes so fiercely that people must cover their faces completely to avoid painful burns. Yet, even while part of one's body feels hot in the sunlight, any part that is in the shade—even if it is only a foot hanging in the shade of the horse on which the traveler is riding—feels as if dipped in icy water.

In all past history this part of the world has been a barrier that no one could cross. It has separated three great civilizations. Those civilizations are today India, China, and the USSR. So one can think of this region not only as a staircase but also as a mighty stone wall. Genghiz Khan came to this wall and could not cross it; so he turned back from India. When Great Britain and Russia were fixing the boundary between their empires toward the end of the nineteenth century, it was decided to keep this wall between India and Russian Turkestan. So a thin strip of land was given to the Afghans to serve as a giant fence of rock and ice. It was of no use to the Afghans, for it is so high that it is difficult to breathe there; but it served as a wall between India and Russia.

The land of the Tadjiks lies just north of this wall. It is at the far southeast of the USSR, the last jumping-off place before you reach the Afghan fence. Tadjikistan is 55,545 square miles in size with somewhat more than 1,000,000 people—that is about half as large as Arizona but about four times as thickly settled. Most of the Tadjiks live on the lower steps of their staircase. They have irrigated land and raise cotton, grapes, apricots, or even sugar cane. Those who live higher up the stairs have very scanty food crops. Those who live near the top have to be shepherds and eat the grass, like the sheep.

Ages ago the Tadjiks had a much more comfortable territory. They were the first known farmers in Central Asia, which is not far from being the first in the world. Their grapes went to China before the Christian era; the Chinese learned from the Tadjiks how to cultivate vines. The Tadjiks were an Iranian people, tall and dark with straight noses and thick beards—a people highly cultured in poetry and music. One conquering race after another took the best lands and pushed the Tadjiks higher up the mountain staircase until they met the Kirghiz on the "roof of the world." Many Tadjiks turned shepherds, like Kirghiz, in order to live.

For all that, the Tadjiks are very different from the Kirghiz. The Kirghiz were always wandering shepherds living in felt tents. But the Tadjiks are so devoted to farming that even when they were driven into barren mountains they carried baskets of earth from the valleys to spread on the rocks and make tiny farms. They are such expert irrigators that even high in the gorges they make wooden pipes to carry water across ravines. They are also expert trailmakers. It is an experience to travel on their mountain trails. They build a trail around a cliff face by sticking logs into breaks in the cliff and covering the logs with brush. The path vibrates with every step and sometimes there are two thousand feet of empty air right under that shaking brush. Tadjiks learned to be good mountaineers; if they weren't they died young on those trails.

For hundreds of years the Tadjiks cut irrigation canals and built trails and developed their giant staircase. In all those centuries they were always ruled by some other race of conquerors. They could never call their country their own. They knew nothing of the progress that went on in the great world beyond

In the Soviet Pamir—young Tadjiks gather for a song at the end of the day

their hills. They kept on farming with the same crooked stick for a plow that was used by Babylonians, the earliest known plow in the world. In many of their upper valleys the people never saw a wheeled cart. The first wheel these people saw was the wheel of an airplane. The airplane brought in carts and these were assembled in the high valleys after the plane had come. This, of course, was after the Revolution of 1917.

Just before the revolution the Tadjiks were ruled by the Emir of Bokhara, who claimed to be the personal representative of Allah but who ran one of the most corrupt regimes on earth. What went on in his harem—where he had scores of beautiful girls and handsome boys—could not be described in a decent book. He supported his luxury and immorality by heavy taxes; the proverb said that he taxed everything but the air. He did not use the public money even to give a water supply to his own capital. Water carriers walked into the stagnant "holy pools" with dirty feet and carried water away in goatskin bags to sell. Many of the carriers were infected with a worm that burrowed under the skin; this infection spread with the water the people used. As for hospitals—there was only one in all the emir's domain. This the emir used for his wives and favorites. There were 8000 sorcerers to cure the ordinary sick.

If the emir thus neglected his own capital, one may imagine how he neglected the Tadjiks—that unimportant people in the mountains. To the emir and to all his officials the Tadjiks were less than the dust.

When the Tadjiks learned that the revolution would get rid of the emir and give even the poorest Tadjik the right to land and to water, they fought for it very heroically. Here is the story of one of them.

This young Tadjik woman has completed a course in typewriting and has an administrative job on the Komintern collective farm

A group of Red Army men was besieged in a fort high up in the Pamirs. They had used most of their food and ammunition. The only place where they might get help was another fort farther down the same river, four days away on horseback. They did not even know if the men in the lower fort were alive or dead. And they couldn't possibly wait four days.

So the commander called a Tadjik skilled in swimming and gave him a letter wrapped in oilskin. "In this packet are our lives," he said. "Don't give it to the tsar or the emir or the bandits but only to a Red commander. Give it to the commander in the fort below if he is living; otherwise to any Red commander you can find."

The river that ran from one fort to the other was full of waterfalls and rapids and whirlpools in which no rowboat or canoe could live. The Tadjik tied two goatskin bags together, blowing them full of air. This is the kind of floating life preserver the peoples of Asia use in crossing rivers. They are somewhat like our water wings. The Tadjik threw himself, with these bags, into the boiling river and was carried rapidly downstream.

Twelve hours later the sentry at the fort below saw a man crawl out of the river. He was badly cut and bruised by the rocks. The sentry challenged him. The Tadjik displayed the oilskin packet and said the only two words he had learned in Russian: "Krasny Kommandir—Red Commander." The sentry tried to take the packet, but the Tadjik refused to give it up in spite of the sentry's threats. Finally the sentry brought him to the commander. The latter was already in desperate straits and was preparing a mine to blow up his entire force rather than be captured and tortured. The message brought by the Tadjik—in twelve hours by water instead of four days by horse—enabled the two forts to combine and win.

This story was only told four years later, when the Tadjik who did not know much about modern methods, was fired from a job and accused of sabotage. To prove his loyalty he hunted up the commander whose fort he had saved. When the story was told, the Tadjik not only got his job back but was decorated by the "Order of the Red Banner."

"Why didn't they give it to him sooner?" I asked when I heard it in Tadjikistan.

"Because nobody in the mountains thought his deed unusual," was the reply.

People like that went ahead very fast when they got the chance. Here is the story of what happened to a Tadjik girl. She was twenty-five years old when she told it. It is the tale of her life.

"We lived on the side of the mountains as our grandfathers lived. We carried earth a long way in baskets to cover the bare rocks and sow a little grain. We got some barley that lasted a few months each year. In spring we gathered a kind of grass that grows in the hills. You dry it and grind it and get something that looks like flour. You mix it with water and bake it in thin cakes. Rich people who had a goat made these grass cakes with milk. There were other kinds of grasses and also roots that we ate.

"I was about ten years old when I spent three days on the cliffs gathering grass. My hands and legs were cut and bruised by rocks. When I came back to the village, some boys knocked me down and took the grass. When I came home without grass, my aunt, with whom I lived, beat me so hard that she came later in the night to see if I were alive or dead.

"When she saw that I was alive she decided to make money from me. Everyone said that I was beautiful. My aunt sold me to an Afghan; that was in 1922 and we lived on the edge of

Afghanistan. My aunt got a lot for me—I thought it was a lot
—two bushels of rice, two bolts of cotton goods, an iron pot,
and an old horse. The horse was the chief thing. Everybody
said: 'What a lucky girl; they gave a whole horse for her!' My
husband took me by night over the border, crossing the river on
a goatskin raft.

"I didn't stay long with this husband. My aunt was pleased
to have got so many nice things for me, so she sent her men relatives to steal me back; then she sold me again, this time to a
carpenter in a near-by village. This time she only got cotton
goods and opium, but my aunt liked opium and was very grateful to the carpenter. This was already 1924 and I had begun
to hear all the new things that were happening, and especially
about the young people's league. I met with them in secret and
learned to read. They told me I did not have to stay with my
master. So I ran away from that carpenter.

"I fell in love with a Russian and he took me to Leningrad.
I traveled with my baby for a whole month in a basket on a
camel. Everything frightened me, especially the train. I fell in
a dead faint when I saw a locomotive for the first time. That was
in 1927, only ten years ago. Now I am a doctor specializing in
childbirth and care of babies. I decided after much thought that
this was the most useful thing to do for my people. And now
that my husband is dead I am going back to my people to take
care of mothers and babies in the hills."

It took several years to restore order in Tadjikistan; for there
is a very long and wild frontier with Afghanistan, and the
emir's followers established themselves on the other side of the
border and attacked in many bandit raids. They were beaten
back after the Tadjik villages became organized for self-
defense. In 1924 when the Soviet Government divided Central
Asia according to nationalities, the Tadjik Republic was formed.

A wheatfield high in the Pamir

A fissure in the Ododi glacier   A log bridge across a stream

In 1929 it became a sovereign state. The Tadjiks at last ruled over their own country for the first time in many hundred years.

After that the country went ahead very rapidly. Water was made public property, used by all the people on equal terms. Old irrigation canals were improved and new ones made. The total cultivated area reached 2,500,000 acres in 1940. This is not large in comparison with some of the bigger republics, but it is twice what the Tadjiks had in pre-Soviet days. Every Tadjik is proud of the first big dam that was built on the Vakhsh River, irrigating 250,000 acres of new land and restoring the irrigation of an even larger area. The Tadjiks know very little about the distant United States of America, but they like to boast that while their Vakhsh Canal used twenty-six excavators the great Panama Canal used only seventeen.

Crops flourish today on all the steps of the giant staircase. In the frostless lower valleys they harvest the fine Egyptian long-staple cotton; the yield has more than tripled with better equipment and methods. Farther up are 40,000 acres of vineyards and 125,000 acres of orchards, yielding rich crops of apricots, figs, almonds, cherries, and plums. On higher steps they grow grain. Even the desolate "roof of the world" now produces scientifically adapted food crops; the first were sown in 1933.

In that same year 300 geologists visited this high region. They carried on work throughout the summer, some of it at heights of 16,500 feet above sea level—2000 feet higher than Pikes Peak or Mt. Rainier. They found many valuable minerals, including a great belt of gold—the highest gold field in the world. Since that time there have been many expeditions. Right across the "roof of the world," where in 1929 I followed a thin caravan track marked with the white bones of dead camels, a motor highway runs.

On the base of new minerals and increased farm products new industries have begun. In 1913 there were only 204 industrial workers in the entire area; there were more than 20,000 in 1938.

Only one person in two hundred could read before the revolution. Today there is compulsory education. There were 257,240 pupils in schools in 1938, about one-fourth the population. Formerly there were neither doctors nor nurses; now there are 144 hospitals and 797 clinics. Fifty-eight newspapers and six magazines are published in the Tadjik language. There is also a Tadjik branch of the Academy of Sciences.

High up in the hills, scientists discovered an old ruined castle containing manuscripts of a civilization that flourished 2500 years ago. These finds have made it possible to restore the ancient language and learn the way of life in very early days.

The Tadjik scientists are also thinking of the future. A remarkable lake has appeared which is both more dangerous and more full of promise than the lake of the Buddhist monk where

The yak is a common animal in the eastern Pamir—Tadjiks use its milk, wool, hide and meat

the "dragon" dwelt. This new lake came into existence as the result of an unusual earthquake. On a February night in 1911 a mountain toppled and fell into a river, shaking all Central Asia with its fall. Behind the natural dam made by the mountain the river slowly rose and formed a lake. This lake is now fifty miles long and two-thirds of a mile deep. It is still growing. It threatens someday to smash through the mountain. This would wipe out hundreds of miles of farms and villages, almost half of Tadjikistan.

Tadjik scientists propose to prevent this by building a man-made dam, equal in size to the great Dnieper Dam. They are carefully watching the growing lake and noting its pressures, which are not yet very dangerous. Meanwhile they make plans for this monster power dam, which will give light and power for a fully industrialized Tadjikistan.

"You have resurrected peoples from the dead, peoples who were less than the dust," said the Tadjik poet Lahuti to Stalin when he visited Moscow with a delegation of record-making Tadjik cotton growers. "Now these people have conquered the earth and have come to report their victory."

"The past was a stairway of years carpeted with pain," said Arith Shakirov, one of the cotton growers. "The Uzbeks feared to go along the street of the Arabs; the Tadjiks carried sticks when they walked through the Uzbek quarter. Hardly anyone could read. That past is gone. On its ruins we build a bright new life. Woe unto anyone who tries to take it away from us."

THE WAR OF THE WHOLE PEOPLE

AT DAWN ON June 22, 1941, the armies of Adolf Hitler struck at the USSR in a surprise attack. Thousands of German planes bombed Soviet cities before the Soviet people knew that a war was on. Thousands of tanks smashed over the frontier followed by millions of motor-borne troops.

The Germans came fresh from the conquest of Europe. They had superiority in men and machines. They drove the Red Army back and advanced a long distance into the USSR in the first few days of war. They expected the fall of Moscow in a matter of weeks.

In the first ten days of war the Soviet High Command estimated the German striking power and devised the counterstrategy. Stalin announced it to the Soviet people in a radio speech at dawn on July 3. He called this strategy a "war of the entire Soviet people." Then he proceeded to explain.

The Red Army must make a slow, hard-fought retreat. It must "fight for every inch of Soviet soil." All war industries must speed up their work for the front. All citizens must work for the war with "daring, initiative, and intelligence," tolerating no thought of defeat. If the enemy conquered territory he must find nothing of value in it. Rolling stock of railroads, factory equipment, cattle, grain, and farm machinery must all be moved east. Anything that could not be taken must be destroyed lest the enemy use it to strengthen himself. In regions held by the Germans the people must make life unbearable for the enemy by sabotage and guerrilla warfare.

"In this great war we shall have loyal allies in the people of Europe and America," Stalin declared. "Our war for the freedom of our country will merge with the struggle of the peoples of Europe and America for their independence, for democratic liberties. . . . All forces of the people for the smashing of the enemy!"

This was not a political speech of patriotic phrases. It was an announcement of the strategy that finally beat Hitler. It was a strategy combining the Red Army, the farms and factories, and all civilian activities in a common plan. It was a strategy to use the Soviet people's total capacity.

The German General Staff had correctly estimated the Red Army. It sent against the USSR 179 German divisions, while its allied troops from Italy, Rumania, Hungary, and Finland brought the attacking force to 240 divisions. The German army was stronger than the Red Army in men and machines, especially in tanks. The Germans had a famous blitzkrieg tactic—penetrating the opposing line by one overwhelming blow and spreading rapidly through the "soft" civilian rear. This tactic had quickly conquered every country against which it had been tried. The Germans were seasoned and confident with successes. They had the advantage of the surprise attack. They had behind them enormous war supplies obtained from the collapse of Europe. They had Europe's armament works and Europe's steel production—50,000,000 tons against 20,000,000 in the USSR. These were the factors on which all the military experts reckoned, in predicting swift collapse of the USSR.

This was the handicap that Stalin's strategy set out to overcome. The German generals had estimated the Red Army, but they had not estimated the total capacity of the Soviet people. Nazis, despising the common man, could not even imagine the heroism of farmers and factory workers. Stalin staked everything on mobilizing this total capacity of ordinary people. This strategy was unbelievably costly to the Soviet people. But it was successful. It wore the Germans down until the Red Army was able to drive them out. This strategy causes many military experts to consider Stalin one of the great military leaders of history.

The first surprise of the war to the military experts was the "defense in depth" that the Red Army opposed to Hitler's famous blitzkrieg. When the terrific blow of the panzer columns broke through the front lines of the Red Army, it found no "soft" civilian rear. The tanks met a "hard" rear of civilians organized around their army. Every city was a fortress, every farm and village an ambush. The "broken" front line was not demoralized; it closed again, separating the tanks from their supporting infantry. Thus the blitzkrieg failed and the Germans were forced to a much longer war.

The Red Army's flexibility next surprised the experts. Tremendous bodies of Red Army troops were surrounded by the first German advance. By military theory they were "entrapped" and should surrender. Instead of this they fought on in the German rear. Some of these "lost" divisions fought their way back to the main line after amazing adventures. Others split into small units, becoming guerrilla bands.

The first comments of the Berlin press were on the "mad valor" of the Russians. These "daredevils" did not fight "proper war." Russian tank drivers drove straight into German tanks, overturning them by head-on collision. Russian pilots had a technique for sawing off the enemy's tail with their whirling propellers. Russian defenders of forts continued the fight from room to room, then blew themselves up with the enemy. Russian infantrymen attacked tanks with bottles of gasoline known as "Molotov cocktails."

By a strange irony the first Red Army men mentioned in the Berlin press for "insane valor" were not Russians but Kalmucks, a sheepherding folk from the Volga delta who have been pushed about by different conquerors for a thousand years. The Nazi "superior race" had to admit that for some odd reason this very "inferior race" had produced heroes in the great art of war.

As the war went on, it became clear to everyone that Stalin had somehow managed to make heroes out of a lot of different peoples who had previously been despised. More than that—he had made them loyal to the Soviet Union, willing to fight and die alongside Russians whom they had hated some twenty years before. The Germans had to fight not only the Russians; they were fighting all the sixteen Soviet nations, acting as one.

Here was an Uzbek farmer seventy years old. He sent six sons to the front and himself took over a tractor. Here was a sixty-two-year-old Ukrainian worker who became such a famous guerrilla that he was made "Hero of the Soviet Union"; the Germans put a price of half a million marks on his head. Here was a twenty-year-old Moldavian guerrilla who mined and derailed ten German troop trains, killing a total of 20,000 men. Twenty Armenians won the title "Hero of the Soviet Union"; thirty Armenians were generals.

Women also were fighting. Most of them went to the front as nurses, but some became snipers, machine gunners, pilots. A schoolteacher named Yevdokia became a night bomber, making 354 flights. A thin little Ukrainian girl named Nina defended Odessa and then Sevastopol as machine gunner, killing 500 Germans before she herself was killed. A street in the northern city of Nevel bears the name of a Kazakh girl machine gunner, Mametovka, in memory of the heroism with which she died for that town.

Even children were fighting. In Moscow the small boys competed in tossing incendiary bombs off the roofs. In the occupied districts their exploits were more dangerous. One eight-year-old girl was seriously wounded when she shouted to warn a Red Army man of the presence of a German paratrooper. Another young girl ran through a hail of German bullets and threw herself under a Soviet tank to warn the Red Army that the road was mined. Twelve-year-old Anatoli went to the woods to join the guerrillas; a year later he organized his own gang of "young avengers," who fought thirty-five Germans and killed sixteen. Anatoli lost a leg and was taken to a children's hospital, because he was under fourteen.

German generals recognized the war potential of Soviet children. Field Marshal von Kluge issued an order: "Any little boys caught on the railway lines are to be shot on the spot!"

Hitler's schedule was upset, but his armies kept on rolling. They encircled Leningrad, the fortress city of the north. They looted Kiev, the historic Ukrainian capital. By December of 1941 they held the rich Ukraine and were assaulting the gates of Moscow. But they had lost many months; they came too late.

Modern cities have not been expected to defend themselves.

Civilians have not been trained to fight. Paris declared itself an "open city"; when the Germans had defeated the French army they just walked in. The mayor of Warsaw surprised the world by fighting after the Polish generals and government had fled. The modern world had almost forgotten how mighty a city, with its citizens, can be in defense. Stalin had not forgotten. Much of his strategy was based on the self-defense of Soviet cities.

Moscow was a fortress city. It was the hub of the Soviet defense. Moscow has always been strong strategically. It lies in rolling farmlands crossed by woods and swamps. Armies cannot easily approach except by ten main highways that shoot out from Moscow like spokes of a wheel. Eleven railway lines also shoot out from the city, for Moscow is the greatest railway center in the USSR. The lines are joined by the Belt Line railway in the suburbs. These branching railways and highways give great mobility to the city in defense.

Changes in recent years have made in Moscow what is probably the strongest fortress city in the world. A modern fortress does not consist of immovable concrete; the fall of the Maginot Line proved that. A modern fortress demands mobility of great forces under protection. When the people of Moscow widened their boulevards, built their tall apartment houses of reinforced concrete, they built not only a beautiful city but also a fortress through which six to ten columns of tanks and motorized troops could maneuver at forty miles an hour and shoot out from the city in any direction without a traffic jam. These maneuvers were protected by solid rows of apartment houses four stories high.

Moscow's air defense was based on airfields within the city limits; one of the largest fields in Europe, the Hodinka, is four express stops by subway from the Kremlin. Moscow's antiair-

craft shells covered four sky levels. All war supplies were manu-
factured inside the city, the power plant being based on lignite
deposits behind the town.

"I was terrified when I saw from the air those great masses
of working people," said a captured German pilot. He had been
used to bombing panic-stricken civilians.

"To your skis, men of Moscow," arose the new war cry. To
the German superiority in tanks Moscow opposed the Soviet
superiority in skis. Millions of Russians had learned to ski in
recent years. The Russians began a winter offensive. Russian
ski troops swooped forward in snowstorms to appear far behind
the German positions. The first line of advance had a light 46
millimeter gun drawn by nine men on skis. The second line included heavy artillery on sledges. The Red Army had aerosleds
and special tanks with wide treads designed for snow. The German "summer tanks" froze.

In "fortress Moscow" civilians went on an iron diet of 1600
calories, as compared with 2500 in wartime Britain and 3000 in
wartime America. Teachers in the schools were so weak from
hunger that they could hardly rise from their chairs at the end
of the day. All teaching was oral, for the ink was frozen in the
inkwells and the children's hands were too numb to hold pencils.
There was no coal for schools or dwellings. Coal was for the
war industries. There was no electric light in the homes in the
long winter evenings that begin at four o'clock and last till ten
next morning. Electricity was needed to make munitions.

People went home from twelve hours' work in war factories
and stumbled into bed in darkness, merely pulling covers over
their clothes. People who needed special diets or medicines
simply died, for there were not enough medical supplies for
civilians when millions of men were wounded at the front. On
cold winter days you could see people dragging coffins by ropes

along the icy streets; there was no transport for coffins or for anything but the war.

Fortress Moscow proved too strong for the German conquerors of Europe to take.

The Germans had won important victories. They held some of the richest Soviet territory. They had the Ukraine with the fertile soil that produced one-fourth the grain and two-thirds of the sugar of the USSR. They held the great industrial areas of the Dnieper and the Donets Basin, which gave the USSR two-fifths of its pig iron and half its coal. This was the area on which Hitler counted to supply his conquest of the east as far as India. But the Germans could not "cash in" on these victories because of the strategy of the "people's war."

The blowing up of the Dnieper Dam, which startled the world, was only part of this larger strategy. The world's press described it with the words "scorched earth." The Soviet people never used those words. Their aim was not to destroy industries but to move them east. They destroyed only things that could not be moved and that might help the enemy.

As the Germans approached, factory workers in all the industries formed gangs to dismantle machinery; take down doors and window frames; pack, grease, and transport parts. They loaded the machinery on flatcars, while the workers and their families got into boxcars and went east with their machines. A thousand or two thousand miles away, in the Urals, Central Asia, or Kazakhstan, the native peoples received the factories and helped set them up.

"The front is not only where the cannon roars. It is in every workshop, on every farm." Under this slogan men worked several days on end without sleep to save their factories from the Germans and to get them into production without lost time. Buildings that would normally take months to erect went up in a few weeks. Men operated machines in the open air while the

Total war—Leningrad civilians made barracades and trenches for defense—Red Army men assisted farmers in harvesting grain

buildings went up around them. The great Kharkov tank factory never stopped production for a day. While the machines moved east, workers in Kharkov assembled the spare parts left behind and drove these last tanks against the enemy. Before this assembly stopped, the plant was again producing at its new base in the east.

The farmer's job in the war was to save the grain. As the Germans entered the Ukraine a race began for the grain harvest. Teachers, students, and office workers from the city poured out to the farms to help get in the wheat. Even the Red Army harvested grain in lulls between fighting. By September 10, when the Germans reached the rich heart of the Ukraine, 60 per cent of the harvest had been moved to the rear.

Millions of farming people then moved east on special trains or on trucks and tractors. It was a military operation; they went east on the army trains that brought soldiers to the front. One tractor station from the Ukraine was bound for the border of Iran. A long column of seven tractors led the way, followed by truckloads of implements and spare parts. Artillery thundered behind them as they moved over the prairie. Enemy planes bombed them and killed several people. They buried their dead and journeyed on.

After a thousand miles they reached their destination, picked up handfuls of soil and declared it good. A reception committee of local Azerbaidjanian farmers presented them with boxes of seed, saying: "American seed! Americans sent good seed for this good soil." It was seed from American farms sent through the Russian War Relief.

The peoples of all the Soviet nations—Uzbeks, Turkmenians, Kazakhs, Kirghiz, Armenians, Azerbaidjanians—welcomed the refugees as fellow warriors and also as fellow workers and farmers bringing new machines and tools. These refugees were not scattered jobless among alien peoples like the refugees of Europe. They found a full-time job to do for the war. Farms whose men had gone to the front needed workers. They gave the Ukrainian farmers homes, food, garden plots, sometimes even a cow and chickens, not as charity but on credit against future harvest work.

The great task of the rear was the war against hunger. In this war all the school children from the seventh grade upward helped. The Ukraine—breadbasket and sugarbox—was held by the enemy. Other farm regions must make up for the lack. The young men had gone from all these farming regions. Many tractors and trucks and much of the gasoline had also gone for Red Army needs. Women and old people and cripples and children carried on the war against starvation.

Special courses in farming began in the seventh, eighth, ninth, and tenth grades in December, 1941. By February the children were already organized in field groups and were corresponding with the farms that applied for their work. In March the school doctors gave physical examinations, telling each boy and girl what work their health permitted. Schools closed two weeks early and the children went to the farms in June, boys and girls in separate groups under the leadership of teachers.

That summer 3,505,348 children under 150,096 teachers did a total of 108,350,496 days of work on the farms. Even small tots gleaned precious grainheads, saving thousands of tons of food. Lysenko, the plant specialist, organized 500,000 youngsters, besides, to gather potato eyes and plant them, gaining 150,000 tons of potatoes for food. All this work of the children in the "war against hunger" helped win the greater war.

Many farmers, through necessity or choice, remained in the area held by the Germans. The able-bodied went into the woods as "partisans" or irregular warriors, attacking the Germans from the rear. Such fighters are commonly called guerrillas, but these were unlike any previous guerrillas. They had rifles, machine guns, mine throwers, flame throwers; they had infantry, cavalry, artillery, engineers. Some farmer units had their own planes. They used their knowledge of the district against the enemy. They communicated with the Red Army by two-way radio and by messenger plane.

Their tactics show how these farmers had changed from the once-illiterate peasants. One farmer discovered a German field-telephone line, tapped it, and carried the connection across the front to the Red Army so that its officers could listen in on German plans. One group of fighting farmers captured six German planes on the ground by a sudden dawn attack. They destroyed five, but the sixth was flown to the Red Army by a farmer who was an amateur pilot.

A sixteen-year-old farm boy found eight German tanks in a gully. The fighting farmers, coming from their hiding places, investigated and decided that the tanks were out of gas and waiting for a new supply. They attacked in three groups: gasoline throwers, riflemen, and tractor drivers. The first group hurled thirty bottles of gasoline into the four end tanks, setting them aflame. Twelve Germans jumped from the other tanks and were shot by the riflemen. The four tanks captured uninjured were driven away by the tractor drivers.

In a large area surrounded by Germans a Russian farmer wrote a letter: "Let us take food over the lines into starving Leningrad." The letter went from village to village until it collected 3000 signatures. Then the farmers met in their villages and chose their best people to drive the carts. Two hundred cartloads of food were driven into the besieged city. Thirty of the drivers were women. Three weeks later the 200 carts made a second trip.

The Germans still came on. In the second year of war they made their greatest advance. The Soviet line of defense was anchored in the north by Leningrad, in the south by Stalingrad. These cities made military history.

Leningrad was under gunfire for two and a half years. Most of that time it was under siege. The people existed part of the time on five slices of black bread and two glasses of hot water a day—not a mouthful of anything more. On this they worked, made munitions, and fought Germans. More people died of hunger in Leningrad than of German bombs. But they kept their ranks unbroken. The famous composer Shostakovich was an air warden; he threw bombs off the roofs of buildings. Between times he composed his Seventh Symphony, dedicated to struggle and victory. Any person who lived through the siege of Leningrad was given a medal engraved "Leningrad defense."

Stalingrad anchored the southern end of the line. It commands the southern prairies between the Volga and the Caucasus Mountains. Thirty miles of factories lie along the river at Stalingrad. The city is on a plain without natural defense. By taking Stalingrad, Hitler could encircle Moscow from the south; he would also have the road to the Baku oil and to Iran and India.

"Take Stalingrad at any cost" was Hitler's order. German planes dropped leaflets telling the people of Stalingrad that the Germans would have the town on August 25. Day after day 1000 planes and 1000 tanks struck at the city. In mid-September they hurled 2000 tanks and 2000 planes. They cut the city in half . . . into a hundred pieces. More than once Hitler announced that Stalingrad was taken. "Not a building is left intact," a German reporter wrote.

The people of Stalingrad fought from house to house, from room to room. They used rifles, grenades, knives, kitchen chairs, boiling water. When the buildings were gone they fought from cellars and caves. "Every pile of bricks can be made a fortress if there is courage enough" was Stalingrad's motto. Stalin told them: "Every hillock regained gains time. Every day gained may decide the ultimate issue of the battle of Stalingrad."

While the people of Stalingrad fought, fresh reserves of the Red Army surrounded the fighting city in a great pincer movement. Over 300,000 Germans were caught in that trap. On February 2, 1943, they surrendered.

President Roosevelt cabled a congratulation on the "162 days of epic battle." The civilians of Stalingrad and the Red Army had made of that ruined city the turning point in the battle for the world.

So at last the tide turned on the long front of battle and the people began to go back to the lands that the Nazis had held. They began to go back near Moscow in the winter of 1941–42, near Stalingrad in 1942–43, in the Ukraine in 1943–44.

They found a total destruction such as men have not seen in all history except possibly in the ruin wrought by Genghiz Khan. The baffled Germans wreaked a ruthless slaughter on those civilians who prevented their conquest of the world. They slew millions in special gas wagons or by torture. They took 3,000,000 away as slaves. They burned all buildings as they retreated, drove out and slaughtered all livestock.

The Soviet people of all the sixteen republics who had fought at the front and in the rear together fought joyfully now for the great rebuilding. As the Red Army advanced, trainloads of farm machinery followed behind the army. Tractor stations moved back with thousands of tractors. They began plowing to the sound of retreating guns.

The Russian children who came back to Kalinin that first Christmas held a New Year's festival with the Christmas trees that the Germans had abandoned in their barracks. The people of Rostov rebuilt their waterworks, electric system, and street-car lines in six days. The Ivanovo irrigation system, blown up by the Germans and retaken by the Red Army in the winter of 1942–43, was restored to water its 25,000 acres of rice fields for the coming spring.

The returning farmers made dugouts such as were made once on the American plains. All of the untouched eastern republics "adopted" different devastated districts and began a competition as to which could be first rebuilt. Tractors, implements, seed, food, and clothing were sent to the ruined regions as gifts from the eastern farms.

An article in *Pravda* tells how the whole country helped to rebuild Stalingrad:

"Aid to Stalingrad has grown into an enormous movement. Trainloads of building material come in a steady stream from the Gorky region. The Sormovo works has allotted ten tons of sheet iron for roofing. The Molotov auto works has donated 25 ambulance cars, 25 tractors, and 50 motors for harvester combines. Azerbaidjan has contributed 4450 head of cattle and tons of grain, butter, and other foods. In the distant gold fields of the Far East prospectors pledged 72 pounds of gold to buy machinery abroad for Stalingrad.

"Citizens return and find architects, engineers, and teams of highly skilled builders who have come from all over the USSR. Sometimes they are able to repair their own homes; others take up quarters in dugouts. Explosions constantly rend the air as the sappers clear away the mines, of which the Germans left many. Behind them follow citizens.

"The opening of a newspaper stand is an event. When music begins to come out of the loud-speaker, people stop for a moment and stare with tears of happiness.

"The young people's league, which originally built the

Stalingrad Tractor Works, is taking charge of restoration and has mobilized ten thousand young people from all over the country."

In early 1944 Stalin announced on behalf of the federal government that the sixteen constituent republics of the USSR would henceforth have the right to maintain armies and foreign offices of their own. He stated that they had fought so well together that they deserved this final mark of nationhood. People throughout the world speculated on his meaning.

But high in their mountain pastures the Kirghiz were saying: "Twenty-five years ago we had not even an alphabet; now we shall have ambassadors." Under the snowy peak of Ararat the Armenians were saying: "Once we were a great nation; now we are fully a nation again." To all of them it was a sign that out of the terrible loss there was gain.

They knew it also as a task set before them, as if Stalin had said: "You have built well your farms and your factories. You have fought well in defense of our Union. But now it is not enough to build and to fight. Now it is necessary to think. And this thinking must be done by the minds of many people. For this it is not enough that Moscow should plan. It is not even enough that London and Washington should plan. This plan must be made by the minds of all nations and races, by the minds of all the people of farms and factories, by the minds of the mountain pastures and of the great plains. Appoint your ambassadors!"

So the Uzbeks, who broke out of bondage to build the Grand Canal of Fergana, and the White Russians, who fought for three years in the swamps, and the people of the Ukraine, who built the Dnieper Dam and then destroyed it . . . the people of all the sixteen Soviet Republics prepared to appoint their ambassadors and to share in rebuilding the world.

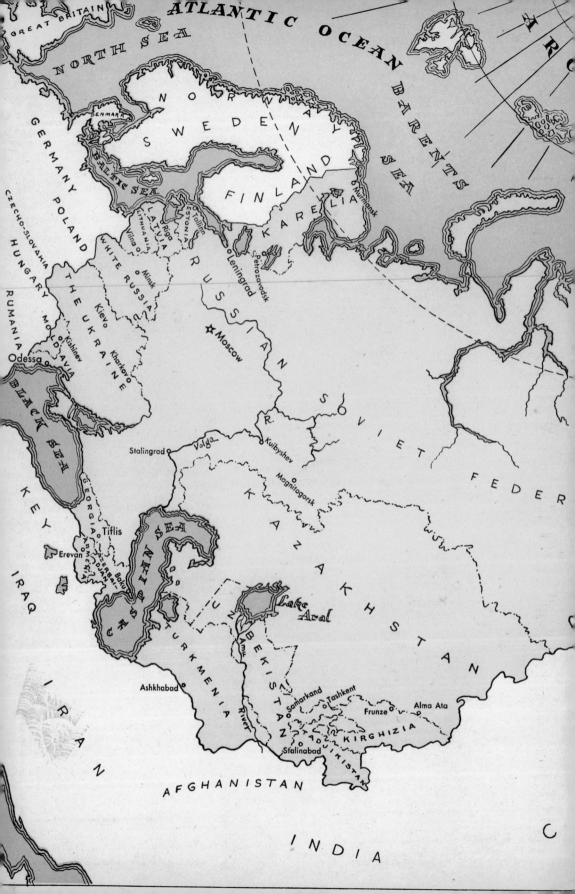